PLAYS FOR PERFORMANCE

*A series designed for
contemporary production and study
Edited by
Nicholas Rudall and Bernard Sahlins*

HENRIK IBSEN

A Doll's House

In a New Translation by
Nicholas Rudall

Ivan R. Dee
CHICAGO

Library of Congress Cataloging-in-Publication Data:
Ibsen, Henrik, 1828–1906
    [Dukkehjem. English]
    A doll's house / Henrik Ibsen ; in a new translation by Nicholas Rudall.
        p. cm. — (Plays for performance)
    ISBN 1-56663-225-0 (alk. paper) — ISBN 1-56663-226-9 (pbk. : alk. paper)
    I. Rudall, Nicholas. II. Title. III. Series.
PT8861.A113   1999
839.8'226—dc21   99-052239

INTRODUCTION

by Nicholas Rudall

Ibsen completed *A Doll's House* in 1879. It is his first truly great work written in conversational prose. He had experimented with this form previously, but most of his earlier work was written in verse and dealt with historical or mythological events.

In a letter to his publisher, Isben had written that he was working on "a play of modern life." In fact he seems to have been inspired, to some extent, by his acquaintance with a woman named Laura Kieler, who was having marital difficulties and contemplating divorce. Not that Laura Kieler was anything like Nora. She was an amibitious woman and a published author. But she seems to have stimulated Ibsen's contemplation on the status of women inside marriage. In the year 1879 there was only one divorce recorded in Norway. So the ideas contained in *A Doll's House* were potentially explosive: the marked inequality of the wife's status and the intellectual arguments that cause Nora to leave. And indeed the play did cause a sensation, not only in Scandinavia but throughout the world. (It was performed in Japan and the United States more than a decade after its publication.) It is still perhaps the one work of Ibsen that finds recurring popularity (often misguided) when sexual politics are dominant in public debate. The final closing of the door

3

of the doll's house as Nora leaves was and is a remarkable theatrical coup that still resonates.

Although *A Doll's House* is a rich character study with enormous psychological challenges for an actor, its basic structure is deeply rooted in nineteenth-century dramatic techniques. It is to a very large extent an example of "the well-made play." This genre, popularized by Scribe and Sardou, had a conventional structure. Typically it was written in three acts. It often included a villain who held some sway over the hero, frequently through the device of a written document, and an obligatory scene in which the dirty secret was revealed but the hero saved. There were of course many permutations of this structure, and the thinness of such plots was often ridiculed and sometimes parodied—for example, Oscar Wilde took great delight in turning the form on its head in *An Ideal Husband.* Ibsen did not exactly embrace the form either. First of all, it should be noted that he had very few *models* of dramatic form that could sustain his foray into psychological realism. But this model of drama allowed him to root his characters in the middle class, eschewing the nobility who had peopled the European stage for so long.

The plot does have a certain predictability, and the twists of circumstance often seem contrived and, well, creaky. Ibsen was clearly aware of the pitfalls. He even has Torvald say to Nora just before the denouement, "Let's have no melodrama here!" And this very predictability is turned into a weapon of surprise in Ibsen's attempt to raise societal issues. Krogstad, the apparent villain, turns out to have a conscience and a desire not to thwart society but to be a part of it. Nora, most surprisingly of all, will not be "saved." She will do the unthinkable. She will leave her family in order to find herself. But what

4

really sets this play off from all its predecessors is not the form but the reality of the feelings and the thoughts of those who are struggling with their lives.

In this series of translations and adaptations, we are committed to providing texts for the contemporary American actor. They are intended to be spoken, though of course this should also make them more accessible to the modern reader. *A Doll's House* differs from some of Ibsen's other conversational prose plays in that the characters are virtually all from the same class (apart of course from the servants). Thus the challenge is not to make distinctions of education or status in their diction but to ensure individuation of their speech patterns. Nora must speak differently from Mrs. Linde and Torvald from Dr. Rank. The distinctions are psychological. For example, Mrs. Linde makes a decidedly meek initial impression but gains in confidence when she finally confronts Krogstad. Ibsen has written a play rich in the polarities of human behavior, and this richness is reflected in the complexity of the spoken word. Although it is set firmly in its own time and place, its themes and its human truths transcend the particular and achieve a moving universality. It is the first great work by the "founder of modern drama."

CHARACTERS

NORA HELMER

TORVALD HELMER, a lawyer and Nora's husband

DR. RANK

MRS. LINDE

NILS KROGSTAD, a bank clerk

THE HELMERS' THREE SMALL CHILDREN

ANNA MARIE, the children's nurse

HELENE, a maid

A DELIVERY BOY

A Doll's House

ACT 1

A comfortable, tastefully but not expensively furnished room. There is a door in the back right wall that leads to the front hallway of the apartment. A doorway on the left leads to Torvald's study. Between the doors is a piano. Halfway down the stage left wall is another door and a window. Near the window is a round table, an armchair, and a sofa. Halfway down the stage right wall is a door and near it a porcelain stove, two armchairs, and a rocking chair. Between the stove and the door is a small table. There are engravings on the walls. There is an etagere with small china figures and objets d'art; a small bookcase with richly bound leather books. There is a carpet on the floor, a fire burning in the stove. It is a winter day.

A bell rings in the hallway. Shortly after, we hear the front door being opened. Nora enters. She is humming happily to herself. She is wearing street clothes and is carrying an armful of wrapped packages, which she puts down on the table. She leaves the hall door open. Through it we can see the delivery boy. He is holding a Christmas tree and a basket, which he hands to the maid who had let them in.

NORA: Hide the tree carefully, Helene. The children mustn't catch a glimpse of it until this evening. Not until we've decorated it. *(to the delivery boy)* How much do I owe you? *(taking out her purse)*

DELIVERY BOY: Fifty pence, ma'am.

11

NORA: There's a hundred. No, keep the change. *(The boy thanks her and leaves. Nora shuts the door and begins to take off her street clothes. She is laughing softly to herself. She takes a bag of macaroons from her pocket, eats a couple, then crosses quietly to Torvald's door and listens carefully.)* Mmm! He's home. *(hums as she crosses to the table)*

TORVALD: *(from the study)* Is that my little lark twittering away out there?

NORA: *(opening packages)* Yes it is!

TORVALD: Is that my little squirrel fussing about in there?

NORA: Yes.

TORVALD: And when did she come home?

NORA: *(putting the bag of macaroons back in her pocket and wiping her mouth)* A minute ago. Do come in, Torvald. Come and see what I've bought.

TORVALD: I'm busy. *(soon after, he opens the door and looks in, pen in hand)* Did you say *bought*? All that? Has Madam Extravagant been throwing money away again?

NORA: But Torvald. . . . This year we should . . . oh, let ourselves go a little. It's the first Christmas we haven't had to count the pennies.

TORVALD: But we can't just go wasting money.

NORA: I know, Torvald. But we can waste just a little bit, can't we? Just a teeny bit? You've got a big salary now . . . you're going to make piles and piles of money.

TORVALD: Yes. After New Year's. And even then it's a full three months before the whole raise comes through.

NORA: Pah! We can borrow money until then.

TORVALD: Nora! *(taking her playfully by the ear)* There you go again! Scatterbrain! Look, what if I borrowed a thousand crowns today and you spent the lot over Christmas, and then on New Year's eve a tile fell off the roof, hit me on the head, and I lay there . . .

NORA: *(hand on her mouth)* Oh! Don't say such things!

TORVALD: Yes, but what if it actually happened—then what?

NORA: If something so terrible happened, I wouldn't care if I had debts or not.

TORVALD: But what about the people I'd borrowed from?

NORA: Them? Who cares about them? I don't know them.

TORVALD: Nora, Nora! Just like a woman! I am serious. Nora, you know how I feel about all that. NO DEBTS. Never borrow! When a home has its foundations built upon borrowing, upon debt, then some part of its freedom, some part of its beauty is lost. Until now we have fought a brave battle, the two of us. And we will keep on fighting for the little while that we still have to.

NORA: Whatever you say, Torvald. *(at the stove)*

13

TORVALD: *(following her)* My little songbird's wings must not droop. Come now. Don't be a sulky little squirrel. *(takes out his wallet)* Nora! Guess what I have here!

NORA: *(turning quickly)* Money!

TORVALD: There, *(handing her some money)* you see? I know how expensive it is to run a house at Christmas.

NORA: Ten, twenty, thirty, forty. Oh thank you, Torvald. I can really take care of everything with this.

TORVALD: Well, you'll have to.

NORA: I promise. I promise. But come and see all that I bought. It was so cheap! Look, some new clothes for Ivar—and a little sword. A horsie and a trumpet for Robert. And a doll with its own little bed for Emmy. They're not very good, but she'll break them to bits in no time anyway. And I bought some dress material and some handkerchiefs for the maids. Old Anna Marie really deserves something better.

TORVALD: And what's in that package there?

NORA: No. Torvald, no! Not until tonight!

TORVALD: I see. But tell me, Little Miss Extravagant, what did you think of for yourself?

NORA: For me? Oh I don't want anything.

TORVALD: Of course you do. Now tell me, what would you really really—within reason of course . . . like to have?

NORA: I honestly don't know. Although, Torvald . . .

TORVALD: Yes?

NORA: *(playing with the buttons on his jacket—but not looking at him)* If you really want to give me something—then maybe—maybe you could . . .

TORVALD: Out with it, come on.

NORA: *(speaking fast)* You could give me money, Torvald. No more than you think you can spare. . . . Then . . . one of these days I'll buy something with it.

TORVALD: But Nora—

NORA: Oh please, Torvald my darling, please. Do that for me. And I could wrap the money in pretty gold paper and hang it on the tree. Wouldn't that be fun?

TORVALD: What do we call those little birds that fly through their money?

NORA: I know. Spendthrifts! Yes, yes, I know. But do what I ask, Torvald, and then I'll have time to make up my mind about what I need most. Now that's sensible of me, isn't it?

TORVALD: *(smiling)* Yes, very . . . if you could actually hang onto the money I gave you and then spend it on something for yourself. But it would go for the house—or something frivolous. And then I'd only have to give you some more.

NORA: Oh but Torvald—

TORVALD: Don't contradict me, Nora. Sweet Nora. . . . Spendthrifts *are* sweet, but they spend an awful lot of money. You have no idea what it costs a man to feed these little birds.

NORA: How can you say that! I save everything I can!

15

TORVALD: *(laughing)* I know, I know. Everything you can. But that adds up to nothing at all!

NORA: *(humming again and with a smile of satisfaction)* Mmmm. . . . If only you knew . . . if only you knew . . . songbirds and squirrels have a lot of expenses.

TORVALD: You're so strange, so like your father. You can find money anywhere and everywhere. But the moment you have it, it runs right through your fingers. You have no idea what you've done with it. Ah well, one takes you as you are. It runs in the blood. It's ingrained—these things arc hereditary, Nora.

NORA: I wish I'd inherited many of Papa's qualities.

TORVALD: And I wish you to be only as you are, my songbird, my sweet little lark. Wait a minute . . . I have the feeling . . . no . . . how should I put it . . . ? You look very guilty about . . . something . . .

NORA: I do?

TORVALD: Yes, you do. Look me straight in the eye.

NORA: *(looking at him)* Well?

TORVALD: *(shaking his finger)* Little Miss Sweet Tooth! Have you been running wild in town again today?

NORA: No. What gives you that idea?

TORVALD: Little Miss Sweet Tooth didn't make a little detour down to the patisserie?

NORA: No. Honestly, Torvald.

TORVALD: Not even a little nibble?

NORA: No. Not a bite.

TORVALD: Not even a macaroon or two . . . ?

NORA: No, Torvald. Honestly, I prom—

TORVALD: It's all right, it's all right . . . I'm only joking.

NORA: I could never deceive you.

TORVALD: I know, I know and you *have* given me your word. *(crossing to her)* Well, keep your little Christmas secrets to yourself. Nora, my darling, I'm sure they'll all be revealed this evening when we light the tree.

NORA: Did you remember to ask Dr. Rank?

TORVALD: No. But there is no need. It is assumed he will dine with us. All the same, I'll invite him when he stops by this morning. I've ordered some superb wine. Nora, you have no idea how much I'm looking forward to this evening.

NORA: Me too! And the children will be so happy, Torvald.

TORVALD: It's such a gratifying feeling . . . to have a safe, secure job . . . a comfortable salary. It . . . it gives one such . . . satisfaction.

NORA: Oh it's wonderful.

TORVALD: Remember last Christmas? For three whole weeks you locked yourself up in your room. Every night. Making flowers for the Christmas tree. Till well past midnight. And other decorations to surprise us. That was one of the most boring periods of my entire life.

NORA: I wasn't bored.

TORVALD: But the results, Nora, were . . . well . . . pretty pathetic.

NORA: Don't bring all that up again. I couldn't help it that the cat tore everything to shreds.

TORVALD: No, it wasn't your fault. You tried so hard to please us all. And that's what counts. But . . . I'm so glad the hard times are over.

NORA: Yes. It's really wonderful.

TORVALD: This year I don't have to sit in my study alone, boring myself to death. And you don't have to tire your precious eyes and your beautiful, delicate hands.

NORA: *(clapping her hands)* No. It's true . . . it's true, Torvald. . . . I don't have to, do I? I love to hear you say that. *(taking his arm)* Now. Let me tell you what I think we should do. Right after Christmas—*(doorbell)* The doorbell! *(tidying the room)* Someone *would* have to come just now. What a bore!

TORVALD: I'm not at home to visitors, don't forget.

MAID: *(from the hallway)* Ma'am, a lady to see you—

NORA: All right, show her in.

MAID: *(to Torvald)* And the doctor's just come too.

TORVALD: Did he go to my study?

MAID: Yes sir, he did.

(Torvald goes back to his room. The maid ushers in Mrs. Linde, who is dressed in traveling clothes, then shuts the door.)

MRS. LINDE: *(hesitant and somewhat dejected)* Hello, Nora.

NORA: *(uncertainly)* Hello . . .

MRS. LINDE: You don't recognize me.

NORA: No. . . . I'm not sure. . . . Wait a minute. . . . It can't . . . Kristine! Is that you?

MRS. LINDE: Yes, it's me.

NORA: Kristine! To think I didn't recognize you! But then . . . how could . . . ? *(in a quieter voice)* You've changed so much, Kristine.

MRS. LINDE: Yes. No doubt I have. It's been nine— ten long years.

NORA: Has it been that long since we last met? Yes. Yes, it has. For me these last eight years have been so truly happy. And so you've come into town too now. Made the long trip in winter. That was brave of you.

MRS. LINDE: The ship got in this morning.

NORA: So you came to enjoy yourself here over Christmas. Of course. That's wonderful! And we *will* enjoy ourselves. But take your coat off. *(helps her)* There now, let's sit here and be warm and cozy by the stove. No, sit in the easy chair. I'll take the rocker. . . . *(takes her hands)* Yes, now you look like your old self again. It was just that first moment. But you look paler, Kristine . . . paler and maybe a little bit thinner.

MRS. LINDE: And much much older, Nora.

NORA: Yes . . . perhaps a bit older . . . a teeny weeny bit older. But not much. *(suddenly serious)* But how thoughtless of me to sit here chattering away. Sweet Kristine, I'm so sorry, so sorry.

MRS. LINDE: What do you mean?

NORA: You lost your husband.

MRS. LINDE: Yes, three years ago.

19

NORA: I knew about it, of course. I read it in the newspapers. Kristine, I meant to write. I really did ... but I kept putting it off ... there was always something ...

MRS. LINDE: Nora, I understand completely.

NORA: No! ... it was awful of me, Kristine. How much you must have suffered. And he left you nothing?

MRS. LINDE: Nothing.

NORA: And there were no children?

MRS. LINDE: No.

NORA: You have nothing then?

MRS. LINDE: Not even a sense of loss. Nothing to ... touch me.

NORA: *(looking incredulously at her)* But Kristine, how could that be?

MRS. LINDE: *(smiling, tired, and smoothing her hair)* Oh, it happens sometimes.

NORA: So completely alone. That must be impossibly hard for you. I have three beautiful children. You can't see them at the moment—they're out with the maid. But you must talk to me, tell me every-thing—

MRS. LINDE: No! No no, tell me about you.

NORA: No, you first. Today I don't want to be selfish. Today it's all about you. But there *is* something I must tell you about. Did you hear about the extra-ordinary good luck we just had?

MRS. LINDE: No, tell me about it.

NORA: Torvald has been made manager of the bank. Isn't that extraordinary?

MRS. LINDE: Your husband? That's wonderful.

NORA: Isn't it? You can't always depend on an income if you're a lawyer . . . especially if you won't go near cases that aren't aboveboard and . . . and honorable. And of course Torvald would never do that . . . and I'm completely behind him on that. . . . Oh we are both absolutely thrilled! He'll start work at the bank right after New Year's, and he'll get a huge salary and lots of commissions. From now on we can live quite differently . . . we can live as we want. Oh Kristine, I feel so happy, so free. Won't it be wonderful to have piles of money and not a care in the world?

MRS. LINDE: Well, it would be wonderful to have enough to meet one's daily needs.

NORA: No! Not just daily needs. But piles and piles of money!

MRS. LINDE: (smiling) Nora! Nora! You still haven't come to your senses! Even at school you just loved to spend money.

NORA: (with a quiet laugh) Yes, that's what Torvald still says about me. (wagging her finger) But this "Nora! Nora!" isn't quite as silly as you all think. We were in no position for me to waste any money. We had to work. . . . Both of us.

MRS. LINDE: You too?

NORA: Yes. I did a few odd jobs—needlework, embroidery, crocheting—that sort of thing (casually) . . . and some other things too. You know that Torvald left his department when we got married? He had no chance of being promoted in his

21

firm. And of course he needed to earn more money. That first year he drove himself so hard. He took on all kinds of extra work. He didn't stop from morning to night. It took its toll. He became deathly ill. His doctors said it was essential for him to go south and travel.

MRS. LINDE: Didn't you spend a whole year in Italy?

NORA: Yes. But it wasn't easy to get away. I'd just had the baby ... Ivar. But we *had* to go. Oh, it was a wonderful trip—and it saved Torvald's life. But it was terrifyingly expensive, Kristine.

MRS. LINDE: I'm sure it was.

NORA: Four thousand eight hundred crowns. That is *so* much money!

MRS. LINDE: It's lucky you had it when you needed it.

NORA: Well, the fact is we got it from Papa.

MRS. LINDE: Oh, I see. That was about the time your father died.

NORA: Yes. Just about then. But I couldn't even go and see him. I couldn't look after him. I had to stay here. I was expecting Ivar, and I had to take care of my poor sick Torvald. Oh my dear Papa! I never saw him again, Kristine. That was the worst time in all my married life.

MRS. LINDE: I know how much you loved him. And then you went to Italy?

NORA: Yes. We could afford it now, and the doctors insisted. We left a month later.

MRS. LINDE: And your husband came home completely cured.

NORA: Fit as a fiddle.

MRS. LINDE: But . . . the doctor?

NORA: Who?

MRS. LINDE: The man who came in with me. . . . I thought the maid called him "doctor."

NORA: Oh! Yes, that's Dr. Rank. But he's not making a house call. He's our best friend. He stops by at least once a day. No, Torvald has been completely healthy since we got back, and the children are strong and fit. And so am I. *(she jumps up and claps her hands)* Oh dear God, Kristine, it's so wonderful to be alive and happy! But how awful of me—here I am talking only about myself. *(sitting on a stool next to Kristine and placing her arms across her knees)* Don't be angry with me. Tell me, is it true that you weren't in love with your husband? Why did you marry him then?

MRS. LINDE: Well, my mother was still alive, but she was an invalid confined to her bed—and I had my two younger brothers to look after. In all good conscience, I didn't think I could refuse his offer.

NORA: No, of course not. Was he a rich man?

MRS. LINDE: I think he was very well off. . . . But the business was precarious, Nora, and when he died everything fell apart and there was nothing left.

NORA: And then—?

MRS. LINDE: Well, I had to scratch out a living somehow. I had a little shop. I did a little teaching and whatever else I could find. The last three years have been work work work without a moment's rest. But it's over now, Nora. My poor mother doesn't need me any more. She's passed on. And my brothers—they've got jobs and are taking care of themselves.

NORA: You must feel so free. . . .

MRS. LINDE: Oh no . . . just unspeakably empty. I have nothing to live for. *(she gets up and is visibly anxious)* That's why I couldn't stand it any more in that godforsaken place. Perhaps it will be easier here to find something to do . . . to occupy my mind. If only I were lucky enough to find a steady job, maybe some office work.

NORA: But Kristine, that would be exhausting. You already look so tired. You'd be far better off going to a health spa.

MRS. LINDE: *(moving to the window)* I have no father to give me money to go traveling, Nora.

NORA: *(getting up)* Oh, don't be angry with me.

MRS. LINDE: *(going to her)* Oh Nora, don't *you* be angry with me! The worst part of this whole situation is all the bitterness stored up inside me. You've got no one to work *for* . . . and yet you've got to grab every opportunity. You have to live . . . and you become selfish. You know when you told me about all your good luck I was happier for myself than for you.

NORA: What do you mean? Oh I see. You thought perhaps Torvald could do something for you.

MRS. LINDE: Yes. Exactly.

NORA: And he will, Kristine. Just leave it to me. I'll bring it up so . . . delicately. I'll find something nice to humor him with. Oh, I can't wait to help you.

MRS. LINDE: You are so kind, Nora, to be thinking of me—more than kind when you know so little about the hardships of this life.

24

NORA: I—? I know so little?

MRS. LINDE: *(smiling)* Well, good heavens, a little bit of needlework and things like that. . . . Nora, you are still a child.

NORA: *(with a toss of her head, she begins to pace)* Well, you don't have to act so superior.

MRS. LINDE: Oh?

NORA: You're like everybody else. You all think I'm incapable of doing anything serious . . .

MRS. LINDE: Oh come . . .

NORA: . . . or of ever having to face the brutality of life . . .

MRS. LINDE: Nora, my dear. You've just been telling me what you've been through.

NORA: Oh, that was nothing. I haven't told you about the really important thing.

MRS. LINDE: The important thing? What was that?

NORA: I'm not surprised that you look down on me, Kristine. But you have no right to. You're proud of yourself because you worked so hard all those years looking after your mother.

MRS. LINDE: I'm not looking down on anyone. But I *am* proud . . . of course, and happy that I know I was able to make my mother's last days a little more comfortable.

NORA: And you're proud of what you did for your brothers.

MRS. LINDE: I think I have every right to be.

NORA: I think so too. But let me tell you something, Kristine. I have something to be proud of too.

MRS. LINDE: I'm sure you do. Tell me about it.

NORA: Keep your voice down. . . . Just think if Torvald were to hear us! He mustn't find out. Not for the world. *No one* must find out. . . . No one but you, Kristine.

MRS. LINDE: Find out what?

NORA: *(pulling her over to the sofa)* Come over here. Oh yes, I've got something to be proud of. It was I who saved Torvald's life.

MRS. LINDE: Saved his life? How?

NORA: I told you about our trip to Italy. Well, Torvald would never have recovered if we hadn't gone there.

MRS. LINDE: Yes. But your father gave you all the money. . . .

NORA: *(smiling)* That's what Torvald thinks, and so does everyone else, but . . .

MRS. LINDE: What?

NORA: Papa never gave us a penny. I raised all the money myself.

MRS. LINDE: You? All that money?

NORA: Four thousand eight hundred crowns. What do you think of that?

MRS. LINDE: Nora! How could you do that? Did you win the lottery?

NORA: *(with a touch of contempt)* The lottery! Pah! How could I be proud of that?

MRS. LINDE: Where did you get it then?

NORA: *(smiling and then humming a little tune)* Aha! Tum tee tum.

MRS. LINDE: Well, you couldn't have borrowed it.

NORA: Oh, why not?

MRS. LINDE: Because it's not possible for a wife to borrow money without her husband's consent.

NORA: *(tossing her head)* Oh, that's not true. . . . Not when a wife has a little talent for business. . . . A wife who knows how to get things done.

MRS. LINDE: But Nora, I don't see how . . .

NORA: No, there's no reason you should. Anyway, I never said anything about *borrowing* the money. There are all kinds of ways I could have got my hands on it. *(stretching back on the sofa)* I could have gotten it from some admirer—after all, I am rather attractive. . . .

MRS. LINDE: Please be serious.

NORA: You really are dying to find out, aren't you, Kristine?

MRS. LINDE: Nora, my dear, listen. You haven't done anything . . . that you might regret?

NORA: How could I regret saving my husband's life?

MRS. LINDE: You might regret that you did something behind his back.

NORA: But I couldn't possibly tell him. Good heavens! Can't you see? It would have been terrible if he had found out how sick he really was. The doctors came to *me* and told *me* that his life was in danger . . . he would only survive if I took him to the South. Well, of course I tried coaxing him to go at first. I told him it would be so nice for me to take a holiday abroad—like other young wives. I tried everything. I cried. I begged. I told him that he had a duty to think of my . . . condi-

27

tion. . . . That he had to be a sweetheart and do what I asked. I dropped hints . . . oh . . . that he could easily borrow the money. Kristine, he nearly exploded in anger. He accused me of being frivolous. He said it was his duty as a husband not to give in to what I think he called my "little whims and daydreams." So I thought to myself, "All right, but your life is going to be saved somehow." Then I thought of a way to do it.

MRS. LINDE: But . . . but your father must have told him that you didn't get the money from *him.*

NORA: No—it was just about then that Papa died. I had always intended to tell him and ask him to keep it a secret. But he was so sick . . . and in the end, well, unfortunately I didn't need to tell him.

MRS. LINDE: And you—you've never told your husband?

NORA: Good heavens, no! How could I? He has such strict rules about these sorts of things. And, well, like most men, Torvald has his pride. He'd feel humiliated—hurt, even—if he thought he was indebted to me in any way. It would spoil everything. This lovely, happy home would never be the same.

MRS. LINDE: Aren't you ever going to tell him?

NORA: *(smiling and thoughtful)* Well, maybe someday. But not for a long time. When I'm no longer pretty. No, don't laugh, what I mean is . . . when Torvald doesn't love me as much as he does now. When he no longer enjoys watching me dancing and dressing up and reciting little poems. It might be a good idea to have that up my sleeve. . . . *(breaking off)* But that's all nonsense. That time will never come. So? Kristine, what do you think of my great secret? I'm not so useless after all? And it hasn't been easy, I can tell you. It's a huge worry to have to meet your obligations on time. In the business world there are things called quarterly payments and installments. They're always so terribly hard to pay on time. So whenever I could, I've scraped together a little bit here, a little bit there. There wasn't much I could save out of the housekeeping money. Torvald has to live a comfortable life, and the children have to look nice. I didn't think I should touch the money I'd set aside for my little sweethearts.

MRS. LINDE: So it all had to come out of your allowance? Oh poor Nora!

NORA: Of course it did. After all, this was my choice. So if Torvald gave me money for a new dress or something, I never spent more than half. I bought the simplest, cheapest things. Thank heavens I look good in almost anything. So ... Torvald never even noticed. But, Kristine, it hasn't been easy. Isn't it nice to be beautifully dressed?

MRS. LINDE: Yes, it is.

NORA: And I found other ways of making money. Last winter I was very lucky. I got a lot of copying to do, and I locked myself away and sat there writing—often till after midnight. Oh, sometimes I got so tired. But, you know, it was so much fun sitting there, working, earning money. It almost felt like being a man.

MRS. LINDE: How much have you been able to pay off?

NORA: Well, I don't exactly know. It's difficult with something like that to know how much you owe. I know this much ... every penny I've made, scraped together, I've paid. Oh God, sometimes I've been at my wit's end. *(she smiles)* I used to sit here and think of some rich old man who'd fallen in love with me . . . and . . .

MRS. LINDE: Who? Who was that?

NORA: Wait . . . and that he died and that in his will in huge letters it said, "All my money is to go to the beautiful Nora Helmer, cash in hand."

MRS. LINDE: But Nora . . . who is this man?

NORA: Oh good heavens, don't you understand? There's no "old man." I just sat here and imagined him . . . oh so many times. I had nowhere to go, nowhere to look for money. But that's all done with now. That stupid old man can stay where he is. I don't care. He's gone and the will is gone. My troubles are over. *(she jumps up)* Oh Kristine, just think . . . nothing to worry about anymore, no more! I can laugh and play with the children. I can buy all the new modern things for the house—which Torvald loves. And soon it will be spring. Blue skies will come back, maybe we'll go away for a little while, maybe we'll see the sea again. Oh, isn't it wonderful to be happy and full of life? *(doorbell rings in the hallway)*

MRS. LINDE: *(getting up)* That's the door—perhaps I should go. . . .

NORA: No, stay. It's for Torvald. They won't come in here.

MAID: *(at door)* Excuse me, there's someone to see the lawyer.

NORA: The bank manager.

MAID: Yes, the bank manager. But I didn't know . . . since the doctor's with him.

NORA: Who is it?

KROGSTAD: *(in doorway)* It's me, Mrs. Helmer.

(Mrs. Linde is startled, collects herself, turns to window)

NORA: *(very tense and in a low voice)* What is it? Why do you want to see my husband?

KROGSTAD: Bank business. In a way. I have a small job in savings at the bank, and I've heard that your husband is to be the new manager, so . . .

NORA: So it's only . . .

KROGSTAD: Only business, Mrs. Helmer, boring business. Nothing else whatsoever.

NORA: Well, he is in his study. *(She gives a brief bow and shuts the door. Then she tends to the stove.)*

MRS. LINDE: Nora, who was that?

NORA: His name is Krogstad. He's a lawyer.

MRS. LINDE: So, it *was* him. . . .

NORA: You know him?

MRS. LINDE: I used to . . . years ago. He worked in a lawyer's office in my hometown.

NORA: Yes, he did.

MRS. LINDE: He's changed.

NORA: He had a very unhappy marriage.

MRS. LINDE: Then he's a widower now?

NORA: Yes, with lots of children. *(she closes the door of the stove and shifts her rocking chair)* There, that should burn well now.

MRS. LINDE: I hear he's involved in all kinds of business deals.

NORA: Really? Well you may have heard right. I don't know anything about... But let's stop talking about business ... it's so boring.

(Dr. Rank comes out of Torvald's study)

DR. RANK: *(in doorway)* No no, my dear man. I don't want to be in your way. And anyway, I'd like to see your wife for a while. *(he shuts the door and notices Mrs. Linde)* Oh, I beg your pardon. I seem to be in the way here too.

NORA: Of course you're not! Dr. Rank—Mrs. Linde.

DR. RANK: I keep on hearing that name in this house! Didn't I pass you on the stairs on the way up?

MRS. LINDE: Yes. I don't like stairs. I have to go very slowly.

DR. RANK: You're not feeling well?

MRS. LINDE: Just tired, I think. I've been working too hard.

DR. RANK: That's all? So you've come to town for a rest? Lots of parties, eh?

MRS. LINDE: I've come to look for work.

DR. RANK: Not a very clever cure for exhaustion.

MRS. LINDE: One has to live, Doctor.

DR. RANK: Yes, current opinion seems to be in favor of it.

NORA: Now, Dr. Rank, you want to live as much as anybody.

DR. RANK: Indeed I do. However terrible I may actually feel, I want to prolong the agony. For as long as possible. My patients all seem to have the same idea. And it even applies to those whose sickness is moral. At this moment there is a man in there with Helmer who's a moral cripple.

MRS. LINDE: *(softly)* Ahhh.

NORA: Who do you mean?

DR. RANK: Oh, you wouldn't know him . . . he's a lawyer by the name of Krogstad. He's a thoroughly rotten human being. But the first words out of his mouth—as if it were important—"Oh, but I have to live."

NORA: Oh, what did he want to see Torvald about?

DR. RANK: I've no idea. I think he said something about the bank.

NORA: I didn't know that Krog . . . the lawyer had anything to do with the bank.

DR. RANK: Yes, he has some sort of job there. *(to Mrs. Linde)* I don't know if the same thing happens in your town, but here there are people who go around sniffing out moral corruption, and when they've found it they *reward* the owner with a well-paid job—just so they can keep an eye on him. An honest man will find himself left out in the cold.

MRS. LINDE: Well, perhaps the sick do need looking after.

DR. RANK: *(with a shrug of his shoulders)* There you are, you see. That's the sort of opinion that's turning society into a home for the diseased.

NORA: *(She has been deep in her own thoughts. She suddenly gives a quiet chuckle and claps her hands.)*

DR. RANK: Why do you laugh at what I said? Do you really understand what society means?

NORA: Oh, what do I care about your boring old society? I was laughing about something else, something very funny. Tell me, Dr. Rank, do all the people who work at the bank have to report to Torvald now?

DR. RANK: Do you find that so "very funny"?

NORA: *(smiling and humming)* Ah . . . that's my business. *(walking around the room)* Well, yes, it really is very funny to think that we—that Torvald has so much power over so many people. *(taking the paper bag from her pocket)* Dr. Rank, would you like a macaroon?

DR. RANK: Macaroons? Well! I thought they were forbidden in this house.

NORA: They are. But Kristine gave these to me.

MRS. LINDE: *(somewhat frightened)* What? I . . . I . . .

NORA: Nothing to be frightened of. You didn't know that Torvald had forbidden them. The fact is, he's afraid they will ruin my teeth. But . . . pah . . . once in a while . . . that's all right, isn't it, Dr. Rank? *(putting one in his mouth)* Here! Have one. And one for you, Kristine. And I'll have one too . . . just a teeny one. No more than two! *(walking about again)* Oh I'm *so* happy! There's just one thing more that I would *love* to do.

DR. RANK: And what is that?

NORA: Something I've been *longing* to say in front of Torvald.

34

DR. RANK: Why can't you say it?

NORA: Oh, I couldn't . . . it's very bad.

MRS. LINDE: Bad?

DR. RANK: Then you'd better not . . . though perhaps in front of *us*? What is it that you'd *love* to say in front of Torvald?

NORA: I'd love to say—Well, I'll be damned!

DR. RANK: You must be mad!

MRS. LINDE: Nora! My dear . . .

DR. RANK: Well, go ahead! . . . he's coming out.

NORA: *(hiding the macaroons)* Sh! Sh! Sh!

(Torvald comes out with his coat over his arm and his hat in his hand)

NORA: *(crossing to him)* So. Torvald, my dear, you got rid of him?

TORVALD: Yes. He's just left.

NORA: Let me introduce you—this is Kristine. She just came into town.

TORVALD: Kristine . . . ? I beg your pardon. . . . I don't remember . . .

NORA: Mrs. Linde, dear. Kristine Linde.

TORVALD: Oh yes. You and my wife were at school together, weren't you?

MRS. LINDE: Yes. That's when we met.

NORA: Just think, she came all this way to see you!

TORVALD: To see me?

NORA: Kristine is extremely good at office work. And she really wants to work for a man who knows what he's doing so she can perfect her skills.

TORVALD: That's a wise choice, Mrs. Linde.

NORA: So when she heard you'd been made manager of the bank—there was a telegram or something—she came here as quickly as she could. You'll be able to do something for Kristine, won't you, Torvald, for my sake?

TORVALD: Well, it's not impossible. . . . I presume you are a widow, Mrs. Linde?

MRS. LINDE: Yes.

TORVALD: And you've had some experience in accountancy?

MRS. LINDE: Yes. A fair amount.

TORVALD: Then it's more than likely I can find a position for you.

NORA: *(clapping her hands)* There you are. Didn't I tell you?

TORVALD: You came at the right moment, Mrs. Linde.

MRS. LINDE: How can I ever thank you?

TORVALD: There's no need . . . *(putting on his overcoat)* But now you must excuse me . . .

DR. RANK: Wait a moment. I'll come with you. *(getting his fur coat from the hall and warming it by the stove)*

NORA: Come back soon, Torvald my dear.

TORVALD: I won't be more than an hour.

NORA: Are you going too, Kristine?

MRS. LINDE: *(putting on her coat)* Yes. I must go. I have to find a room.

TORVALD: Then perhaps we can all walk down the street together.

NORA: *(helping her)* It's such a shame that we don't have more room . . . but we couldn't possibly—

MRS. LINDE: Don't even think of it! Goodbye, my dear Nora. And thank you.

NORA: Goodbye for now—you'll come back this evening, won't you? And you too, Dr. Rank. What? "If you feel up to it"? Of course you will. Wrap yourself up warmly.

(They all go out into the hallway still talking. Then the children's voices are heard on the stairs.)

NORA: Here they are. Here they are!! *(She runs to open the door. Anna Marie, the Nurse, comes in with the children.)* Come on in! Come in! *(she bends down and kisses them)* Oh, my little sweethearts! Look at them, Kristine, aren't they darling?

DR. RANK: Let's not stand here in the draft.

TORVALD: Come along, Mrs. Linde. Only a mother could stand to be here now!

(They go down the stairs. The children, the Nurse, and Nora come back into the room.)

NORA: Oh, you look so nice and healthy. Pink cheeks—like apples! . . . no, like roses! *(the children chatter through the following)* Did you have a good time? Oh that's good! You gave Emmy and Bob a ride on your sled? Both of them? At the same time? Oh my goodness! You're such a big boy, Ivar. Let me take her for a moment, Anna, my little baby doll! *(taking the baby from the Nurse and dancing with her)* Yes. Mummy will dance with Bobby too! What? You played snowballs? Oh, I wish I'd been there. Leave them, Nanny. I'll take their things off . . . let me do it . . . it's such fun. You go off now, Anna Marie, you look half frozen. There's some hot coffee on the stove in there. *(The Nurse goes into the room on the left. Nora takes off the children's outdoor clothes, throwing them on the floor. They keep talking to her all at once.)* What? A big doggie ran after you? But he didn't bite you. No, big doggies don't bite little doll babies . . . Ivar! No! Don't open the parcels. What's inside? Wouldn't you like to know! Oh no, it's nothing nice at all! You want to play a game? What do you want to play? Hide-and-seek? Yes. Let's play hide-and-seek. Bob, you hide first. Me? All right, I'll go first.

(The children and Nora play the game both in the living room and in the room next to it. They are screaming with laughter. Nora hides under the table. The children run about looking but can't find her. Then the sound of her muffled laughter makes them run to the table and lift the cloth and they see her. Lots of shouting. She comes out on all fours trying to mock-frighten them. More shouts. There has been a knocking at the front door. No one has noticed. The door half opens. Krogstad is standing there waiting as the game continues.)

KROGSTAD: Excuse me, Mrs. Helmer . . .

NORA: *(stifles a cry and starts to get up)* Oh! What do you want?

KROGSTAD: I'm sorry . . . but the front door was open. Perhaps someone forgot to shut it.

NORA: *(rising)* My husband is out, Mr. Krogstad.

KROGSTAD: I know.

38

NORA: What do you want then?

KROGSTAD: A word with you.

NORA: Me! *(to the children, gently)* Go in and see Nanny. What? No. The strange man won't hurt mummy . . . as soon as he's gone we'll finish our game. *(She takes the children into the other room and shuts the door. She is tense and wary.)* You want to see me?

KROGSTAD: Yes, I do.

NORA: Today? But it's not the first of the month yet. . . .

KROGSTAD: No. It's Christmas Eve. And it's up to you whether you have a merry Christmas or not.

NORA: What do you want? I can't spare anything today. . . .

KROGSTAD: We'll talk about that later. This is about something else. Perhaps you can spare me a moment?

NORA: Well . . . yes . . . I can . . . but . . .

KROGSTAD: Good. I was sitting in Olsen's restaurant and saw your husband going down the street . . .

NORA: Well?

KROGSTAD: With a lady.

NORA: So . . . ?

KROGSTAD: May I be so bold as to ask if it was a Mrs. Linde?

NORA: It was.

KROGSTAD: She just arrived in town?

NORA: Yes. Today.

KROGSTAD: She's a good friend of yours?

NORA: Yes, she is. But I don't see . . .

KROGSTAD: I knew her too. Once upon a time.

NORA: Yes. I know.

KROGSTAD: Oh? You know about it? I thought so. In that case I can ask you straight out: Is Mrs. Linde going to get a job at the bank?

NORA: How dare you question me, Mr. Krogstad. . . . You, one of my husband's subordinates. But since you ask I will tell you. Yes, Mrs. Linde is going to work at the bank. And it was I who recommended her, Mr. Krogstad. Now you know.

KROGSTAD: Well, that's what I suspected.

NORA: (pacing) So. . . . It seems that I have a little influence. Just because one is a woman doesn't necessarily mean—and a subordinate, Mr. Krogstad, should be careful not to cross anyone who has . . . well . . .

KROGSTAD: Influence?

NORA: Exactly.

KROGSTAD: (changing his tone of voice) Mrs. Helmer, I expect you will be good enough to use your influence on my behalf.

NORA: What do you mean?

KROGSTAD: That you will be kind enough to see to it that I don't lose my subordinate position at the bank.

NORA: What do you mean? Who is proposing to take it away from you?

KROGSTAD: Oh, you don't have to pretend you don't know. I completely understand. . . . Your friend is not particularly keen to come into contact with me again. And I quite understand whom I'd have to thank for being fired.

NORA: But I assure you . . .

KROGSTAD: I'm sure you do. But to come to the point. I think it's time for you to use your influence to make sure that doesn't happen.

NORA: But, Mr. Krogstad! I have no influence!

KROGSTAD: You don't? I thought you just said . . .

NORA: Well, naturally I didn't intend you to think *that's* what I meant. Me? Why would you think that I have any influence of that kind on my husband?

KROGSTAD: Oh, I've known your husband since we were students. I don't think he's less . . . susceptible . . . than other husbands.

NORA: If you continue to speak disrespectfully of my husband, I will turn you out of the house.

KROGSTAD: That's very brave, Mrs. Helmer.

NORA: I'm not afraid of you any more. After the New Year, I will be finished with the whole thing.

KROGSTAD: *(controlling himself)* Now you listen to me, Mrs. Helmer. If necessary I am ready to fight for my little job at the bank as if I were fighting for my life.

NORA: I can see that.

KROGSTAD: It's not just for the money. In fact that's the least important thing. It's something else—I might as well tell you. It's this. I'm sure you know, like everybody else, that some years ago I made an unfortunate mistake.

NORA: I've heard something about it.

KROGSTAD: It never went to trial. But after that, all doors were closed to me. So I turned to the business that brought us together. I had to make a living. And to tell the truth, I haven't been as bad as some others. But it's time for me to be done with all that. My sons are growing up. And for their sake I must regain my reputation in this town. The job at the bank was the first step up for me—and now your husband is going to kick me back down into the mud.

NORA: You must believe me, Mr. Krogstad. I have no power to help you.

KROGSTAD: But if you set your mind to it. . . . You should be aware that I have the means to force you . . .

NORA: Are you threatening to tell my husband that I owe you money?

KROGSTAD: Well, what if I did tell him?

NORA: That would be a totally contemptible thing to do. *(sobbing)* I have kept this from him with pride and with happiness. I could not bear to have him find out like that—from *you*—in such an ugly, clumsy way. It would be terribly unpleasant for me.

KROGSTAD: Just unpleasant? . . .

NORA: *(impetuously)* All right, then—tell him. But it'll be all the worse for you. My husband will see for himself what a monster you are. And there is no way that you will keep your job.

KROGSTAD: I meant—do you think that it would be "unpleasant" for you only at home?

NORA: If my husband does find out, he will of course immediately pay you what is still owed. And then we will have nothing more to do with you.

KROGSTAD: *(moving toward her)* Listen, Mrs. Helmer. Either I have a bad memory or you don't know much about business. I think I have to remind you of a few details.

NORA: What do you mean?

KROGSTAD: When your husband was ill, you came to me to borrow four thousand eight hundred crowns.

NORA: I didn't know where else to go.

KROGSTAD: I promised to get you the money . . .

NORA: Yes. And you did.

KROGSTAD: . . . I promised to get you the money on certain conditions. You were so worried about your husband's health, so anxious to get the money for your trip, that I don't think you paid much attention to the details. So. I think it's appropriate that I remind you. I promised to get the money if you would sign a security bond, which I then drew up.

NORA: And I signed it.

KROGSTAD: Exactly. Underneath your signature was a clause naming your father as security. He was supposed to sign this clause.

NORA: Supposed to? He did.

KROGSTAD: I'd left the date blank. In other words, your father was to enter the date on the day he signed it. Do you remember that?

NORA: Yes. I think so.

KROGSTAD: Then I gave you the document for you to mail to your father? Is that correct?

NORA: Yes.

KROGSTAD: And obviously you mailed it immediately because—oh, just five or six days later—you brought it to me, duly signed by your father. And I gave you the money.

NORA: So? Haven't I been paying it off regularly?

KROGSTAD: Yes. Pretty regularly. But—to get back to my point—you were having a very hard time then, weren't you, Mrs. Helmer?

NORA: I certainly was.

KROGSTAD: Your father was very sick, I believe.

NORA: He was near the end.

KROGSTAD: And he died soon afterward?

NORA: Yes.

KROGSTAD: Tell me, Mrs. Helmer, do you by any chance remember the day he died? The date, I mean.

NORA: Papa died on the 29th of September.

KROGSTAD: That is correct. I've made sure of that for myself. And that's what's so strange. *(producing the paper)* I can't explain it.

NORA: What is strange?

KROGSTAD: What is strange, Mrs. Helmer, is that your father signed this contract three days after his death.

NORA: What? I don't understand.

KROGSTAD: Your father died on the 29th of September. But if you look here, you'll see that he dated his signature "October 2nd." Isn't that strange, Mrs. Helmer? *(Nora is silent)* Can you explain it? *(Nora is still silent)* It's also strange that "October 2nd" and the year aren't in your father's handwriting, though I do think I recognize the hand. Now, of course, that could be explained—your father might have forgotten to date his signature, and someone else might just have guessed the date *before* they knew of his death. Nothing wrong with that. It's the signature that's important. That *is* genuine, isn't it, Mrs. Helmer? Your father really did sign his own name, didn't he?

NORA: *(pauses, then looks him straight in the eye and with a toss of her head)* No, he did not. I signed Papa's name.

KROGSTAD: Mrs. Helmer! You realize that is a very dangerous confession?

NORA: Why? You'll get your money back soon enough.

KROGSTAD: Let me ask you something. Why didn't you mail the contract to your father?

NORA: I couldn't. He was much too sick. If I'd asked him for his signature, I'd have had to tell him what the money was for. And in his condition, I couldn't tell him my husband was deathly ill. I couldn't possibly.

KROGSTAD: It would have been better for you if you'd canceled the trip.

NORA: That was impossible! That trip was to save my husband's life. I couldn't cancel it.

KROGSTAD: But did it never occur to you that you were deceiving me?

NORA: Why should I worry about that? I wasn't thinking about you at all. I hated the way you handled everything—so coldhearted, making everything so difficult—even though you knew how desperately ill my husband was.

KROGSTAD: Mrs. Helmer. It's obvious that you don't understand what it is that you are guilty of. Just let me tell you about what *I* did—the thing that ruined my reputation. It was nothing more and nothing worse than what you did.

NORA: You? Are you trying to tell me that *you* would have had the courage to try to save your wife's life?

KROGSTAD: The law doesn't care about motives.

NORA: Then the law is stupid.

KROGSTAD: Stupid or not, it is the law that will judge you if I produce this paper in court.

NORA: I don't believe it. Is a daughter not allowed to protect her dying father from worry and care? Is a wife not allowed to save her husband's life? I don't know much about the law. But I'm sure that there must *be* laws that allow things like that. You are a lawyer. You must know about laws like that. You must be a very poor lawyer, Mr. Krogstad.

KROGSTAD: Perhaps. But when it comes to business— the kind of business you and I have engaged in— don't you think I know about that? All right. Do as you like. But I tell you this. If I lose my job again, I'll bring you down with me. *(he bows and exits)*

NORA: *(she seems buried in thought for a short time, then tosses her head)* That's nonsense! He's just trying to frighten me! I'm not so stupid as he thinks. *(she starts clearing up the children's things)* And yet—? No, it can't be true. I did it because I love my husband.

THE CHILDREN: *(in the doorway, sharing the conversation)* Mother, the strange man has gone out through the front gate.

NORA: Yes, sweethearts, I know. But don't tell anyone about the strange man. Do you hear me? Not even Papa.

CHILDREN: No, Mother. Let's go play!

NORA: No, not now.

CHILDREN: But, Mama, you promised!

NORA: Yes, but I can't now. Run on in. . . . I've got such a lot to do. Off you go, my sweethearts! *(She shuttles them into the room one by one, then shuts the door. She sits on the sofa and starts doing some needlework, but soon stops.)* No! *(she throws down the needlework, gets up, goes to the hall door, and calls out)* Helene? Bring the tree in! *(goes to the table on the left, opens a drawer, and then stops)* No! No! It can't be true!

MAID: *(coming in with tree)* Where shall I put it, Madam?

NORA: Here. In the middle of the room.

MAID: Can I get you anything else?

NORA: No, thank you, I've got everything.

(Maid exits)

NORA: *(starting to dress the tree)* I'll put a candle here—flowers there—oh, that awful man! Everything's fine. The tree will look beautiful. I'll do everything I can to please you, Torvald—I'll sing for you, dance for you. *(Torvald comes in with some papers under his arm)* Oh, are you back already?

TORVALD: Yes. Was anyone here?

NORA: Here? No.

TORVALD: That's strange. I saw Krogstad leaving by the front gate.

NORA: Oh, did you? Oh yes, I forgot. Krogstad was here for a short while.

TORVALD: Nora . . . I can see from your face that he's been here, begging you to put in a good word for him.

NORA: Yes.

TORVALD: And you were supposed to make it seem like it was your idea. You were to hide the fact that he'd been here. Isn't that what he asked you?

NORA: Yes, Torvald. But . . .

TORVALD: Nora, Nora. And you would agree to something like that? Even to have a conversation with a man like that, to promise him anything? And on top of everything, to lie to me?

NORA: Lie?

TORVALD: Didn't you just say that no one had been here? *(shaking his finger at her)* My little songbird must never do that again. A songbird must sing with a pure voice—no false notes. *(putting his arm around her waist)* Isn't that right? Yes, I know it is. *(letting her go)* We'll say no more about it. *(sitting down by the stove)* How warm and cozy it is in here. *(going through his papers)*

NORA: *(after a short pause, during which she dresses the tree)* Torvald?

TORVALD: Yes?

48

NORA: I am *so* looking forward to the fancy dress ball at the Stenborgs the day after tomorrow.

TORVALD: And I am "*so*" curious to see how you're going to surprise me.

NORA: Oh, I've been so very silly.

TORVALD: What do you mean?

NORA: I can't think of anything to wear! Everything seems so silly and unimportant.

TORVALD: Ah. Does my little Nora finally realize that?

NORA: *(standing behind his chair with her hands on the back of it)* Are you very busy, Torvald?

TORVALD: Well—

NORA: What are all those papers?

TORVALD: Bank business.

NORA: Already?

TORVALD: I asked the retiring manager to give me the authority to make the necessary changes in staff and to reorganize the workload. I have to spend Christmas week doing that. Everything has to be ready for the new year.

NORA: Was that why this poor man, Krogstad—

TORVALD: Hmm.

NORA: *(leaning against the back of the chair and stroking his hair)* If you weren't so busy, I'd ask you a really big favor, Torvald.

TORVALD: What? Tell me.

NORA: You have the best taste of anyone I know. And I do want to look nice at the fancy dress ball. Tor-

49

vald, couldn't you help me decide what I should go as, what sort of dress I should wear?

TORVALD: Aha! So the stubborn little lady needs someone to come to her rescue?

NORA: Yes, Torvald. I can't do a thing without you.

TORVALD: All right, I'll think it over. I'm sure we'll come up with something.

NORA: That's so sweet of you. *(Going to the Christmas tree. Short pause.)* The red flowers look really pretty. Tell me, did Krogstad do something very bad?

TORVALD: He forged someone's name. Have you any idea what that means?

NORA: Isn't it possible that he had no choice?

TORVALD: Yes. But in many cases like this, it was probably—indiscretion. I'm not without compassion. I won't condemn a man altogether just because of one mistake.

NORA: I know you wouldn't, Torvald.

TORVALD: There have been many men who have been rehabilitated if they confess their faults and take their punishment.

NORA: Punishment?

TORVALD: But Krogstad did nothing of the kind. He got himself out of it by trickery. And that is why he is now completely ruined.

NORA: Do you think it would—

TORVALD: *(interrupting)* Just think how a guilty man like that has to lie and be a hypocrite with everyone, how he has to put on a false mask even in front of those he loves, even in front of his own wife and children. And the children—that's the worst thing of all, Nora.

NORA: How?

TORVALD: Because an atmosphere of lies infects and poisons the entire household. Every breath the children take is filled with the germs of evil.

NORA: *(coming near to him)* How can you be sure of that?

TORVALD: My dear, I've seen it many times in my career as a lawyer. Most of the people who get into trouble early in life have had a mother who lies and cheats.

NORA: Why do you only say the mother?

TORVALD: It usually seems to come from the mother's influence, although of course a lying father would have the same effect. All lawyers are familiar with the scenario. This man Krogstad has been consistently poisoning his own children with his lies and deception. That is why I say that he is a moral degenerate. *(holding out his hands to her)* And that is why my sweet little Nora must promise not to speak on his behalf. Give me your hand on it. Come on, what's this? Give me your hand! There now, that's settled. I can assure you it would be quite impossible for me to work with him. I literally feel physically sick in the presence of such people.

NORA: *(taking her hand out of his and going to the other side of the Christmas tree)* It's so hot in here. And I have so much to do.

TORVALD: *(getting up and putting his papers in order)* Yes. I must try to get through some of these before dinner. And I must think about your fancy dress too! Oh, and maybe I have a little something wrapped in gold paper to hang on the tree. . . . *(patting her on the head)* My sweet little songbird. *(he goes to his room and shuts the door)*

NORA: *(after a pause, whispering)* No. It can't be true. It can't be. It can't be.

(Nurse opens the door on the left)

NURSE: The children are pestering me to let them come in and see their Mama.

NORA: No. No. Don't let them come in to me. Stay with them, Anna.

NURSE: Very well, Madam. *(she shuts the door)*

NORA: *(her face pale with fright)* Corrupt my little children? Poison my home? *(short pause, then, with a toss of her head)* It's not true. It can't possibly be true.

ACT 2

The same setting as Act 1. But the Christmas tree is now in the corner by the piano, stripped of its ornaments and with burned-down candles on its somewhat tattered branches. Nora's cloak and hat are lying on the sofa. She is pacing the room, visibly uncomfortable. She stops by the sofa and picks up her cloak.

NORA: *(dropping the cloak)* Is that someone coming? *(goes to the door and listens)* No—there's no one there. Nobody will come on Christmas day—or tomorrow either. But perhaps— *(opens the door and looks out)* There's nothing in the mailbox. It's empty. *(reentering the room)* Nonsense! Of course he can't be serious. It just couldn't happen. . . . No! I have three small children.

(the Nurse enters from the room on the left with a big cardboard box)

NURSE: I finally found the box with the fancy dress.

NORA: Thanks, put it on the table.

NURSE: It's badly in need of repair.

NORA: I'd love to tear it into thousands of little pieces.

NURSE: Good heavens! It can easily be put right with a little bit of patience.

NORA: Yes. Well, I'll go and get Mrs. Linde to give me a hand with it.

NURSE: Going out again? In this weather? You'll catch your death of cold, Madam.

NORA: Worse things could happen. How are the children?

NURSE: The poor little dears are playing with their Christmas presents, but—

NORA: Are they asking for me all the time?

NURSE: Well, they're so used to having their Mama with them. . . .

NORA: Well, Anna, I won't be able to be with them as much any more.

NURSE: Oh well, little children get used to everything.

NORA: Do you think so? Do you think they'd forget their mother if she went away for good?

NURSE: Good heavens. . . . Went away for good?

NORA: I want you to tell me something I've often wondered about—how did you have the heart to give your child away to people you didn't know?

NURSE: I had no choice—if I was to be my little Nora's nanny.

NORA: Yes, but how could you be *willing* to do it?

NURSE: Well, I was going to get a good position, wasn't I? A poor girl who's got into trouble should count herself lucky. Besides, that terrible man wasn't going to do a thing to help.

NORA: I expect your daughter has forgotten all about you.

NURSE: No. Indeed she hasn't. She wrote to me when she got confirmed and when she got married.

NORA: *(putting her arms around her neck)* Dear old Anna Marie, you were such a good mother to me when I was a little girl.

NURSE: Well, my poor little Nora had no other mother but me.

NORA: And if my little ones had no other mother, I'm sure you'd—oh what nonsense I'm talking. *(opening the box)* Go in and see them—. Now I have to—you'll see tomorrow how beautiful I will look.

NURSE: I know there'll be no one more beautiful than you at the ball. *(goes into the room on the left)*

NORA: *(starts to unpack the box, then pushes it away)* I wish I were brave enough to go out. Oh, I hope nobody comes. I hope everything will be all right here at home. Oh what nonsense! Nobody'll come. I just mustn't think about it. Let me brush the muff. Oh what beautiful, beautiful gloves. Stop thinking about it. Stop! One, two, three, four, five, six . . . *(she gives a little scream)* There's someone coming! *(starts for the door, then stands uncertainly)*

(Mrs. Linde enters from the hall, where she has taken off her cloak and hat)

NORA: Oh it's you, Kristine! There's no one else outside, is there? How nice of you to come.

MRS. LINDE: They told me you were asking for me.

NORA: Yes, I was just passing by. As a matter of fact, there is something you could help me with. Sit down by me on the sofa. Look at this. Tomorrow night there's a fancy dress ball upstairs at the Stenborgs. Torvald wants me to go as a Neapolitan fishergirl. He wants me to dance the tarantella that I learned in Capri.

MRS. LINDE: I see. So you're going in character.

NORA: That's what Torvald wants. Here's the dress. Look. Torvald had it made for me there. But it's torn, and I have no idea—

MRS. LINDE: Well, we can easily fix that. Some of the trimming has come loose here and there, that's all. Needle and thread? Now then, that's all we need. *(starting to sew)* So. You're going to be all dressed up tomorrow, Nora. I'll tell you what—I'll pop in for a moment to see you in all your finery. Oh, I forgot to thank you for a wonderful evening yesterday.

NORA: *(gets up and crosses the room)* Well, I don't think yesterday was all that wonderful. You should have come to town a little bit sooner, Kristine. But Torvald really knows how to make a house look beautiful.

MRS. LINDE: And so do you. You're not your father's daughter for nothing. But tell me, is Dr. Rank always as depressed as he was last night?

NORA: No, last night it was very noticeable. I have to tell you—he's got a life-threatening disease. It's a form of consumption—and it affects his spine. Oh the poor man. His father was a terrible creature who lived a life of excess—and his son was sickly from childhood—do you understand what I mean?

MRS. LINDE: *(putting down her sewing)* My dear Nora, how do you know about such things?

NORA: *(walking about)* Ah, when you've had three children as I have, well, people drop by, married women—and they know quite a bit about medical problems—and they talk—about one thing and another.

MRS. LINDE: *(Resumes her sewing. A short silence.)* Does Dr. Rank come here every day?

NORA: Every day. He's Torvald's best friend, and a good friend of mine too. He's just like one of the family.

MRS. LINDE: But tell me—can he be trusted? I mean, isn't he the sort of man who is always eager to please?

NORA: Not in the least. What makes you think that?

MRS. LINDE: Well. When you introduced me to him yesterday, he said that he had often heard my name mentioned in this house. But afterward I noticed that your husband hadn't the slightest idea who I was. So how could Dr. Rank . . . ?

NORA: You're quite right, Kristine. Torvald loves me so much that he wants me all to himself. That's what he says. Early on, he seemed, well, jealous if I even mentioned the people I was so fond of at home. So naturally I stopped doing that. But I often talk about things like that with Dr. Rank because he likes to listen to me.

MRS. LINDE: Now you listen to *me,* Nora. You're still almost a child in many ways. I'm a little bit more mature, a little bit more experienced. I must tell you this—you ought to put a stop to this with Dr. Rank.

NORA: Put a stop to what?

MRS. LINDE: Two things, I think. Yesterday there was some silly talk about a rich admirer who would leave you money—

57

NORA: An admirer who doesn't exist. Unfortunately. What else?

MRS. LINDE: Dr. Rank is a wealthy man?

NORA: Yes, he is.

MRS. LINDE: And he has no dependents?

NORA: No. No one, but . . .

MRS. LINDE: And he comes here every day?

NORA: That's what I said.

MRS. LINDE: How could a gentleman be so tactless?

NORA: I don't understand what you mean.

MRS. LINDE: Don't pretend, Nora. Do you think I can't guess who lent you the four thousand eight hundred crowns?

NORA: Are you out of your mind? How could you think that? A friend of both of us who comes here every day? Can't you see how terribly awkward that would be?

MRS. LINDE: It's really not him?

NORA: No. Absolutely not. It would never have entered my head for a moment. Besides, he had no money to lend at the time. He inherited it afterward.

MRS. LINDE: Well, Nora, that was lucky for you, I think.

NORA: No, it would never have entered my head to ask Dr. Rank. Although I'm quite sure that if I had asked him—

MRS. LINDE: But you wouldn't—?

NORA: Of course not. There's no need as far as I can see. . . . But I'm quite sure that if I told Dr. Rank—

MRS. LINDE: Behind your husband's back?

NORA: Well, I have to put a stop to things with the other person—and *that* will be behind his back. I *must* put a stop to it with him.

MRS. LINDE: Yes. That's what I told you yesterday, but—

NORA: *(pacing)* It's so much easier for a *man* to put things like that right—

MRS. LINDE: One's husband, yes.

NORA: Nonsense. *(stops pacing)* When you pay off a debt you get your contract back, don't you?

MRS. LINDE: Yes. That's the normal procedure.

NORA: And you can tear it up into thousands of pieces, and throw it on the fire—nasty filthy piece of paper.

MRS. LINDE: *(puts down her sewing and, looking Nora straight in the eye, gets up slowly)* Nora, you're hiding something from me, aren't you?

NORA: Do I look as if I were?

MRS. LINDE: Something has happened since yesterday morning. Nora, what is it?

NORA: *(crossing to her)* Kristine— *(stops and listens)* Sh! Torvald just came back. Do you mind going into the children for a moment? Torvald hates to see sewing things in this room. Let Anna Marie give you a hand.

MRS. LINDE: *(gathering up some of the things)* Of course. But I'm not leaving here until we've had this out with each other. *(she goes into the room on the left just as Torvald comes in)*

NORA: *(crossing to him)* I've missed you so much, Torvald.

TORVALD: Was that the dressmaker?

NORA: No, it was Kristine. She's helping me mend my dress. You'll see, I'll look really pretty.

TORVALD: Wasn't that a good idea I had?

NORA: Wonderful. But don't you think it's nice of me to do what you want?

TORVALD: Nice? To do as your husband wishes? You little scamp! But I'm sure you didn't mean it like that. But . . . I mustn't disturb you. You'll want to be trying on your dress, I'm sure.

NORA: You're going to be working?

TORVALD: *(showing her a bundle of papers)* Yes, look at this. I've just been to the bank. *(going into his room)*

NORA: Torvald!

TORVALD: Yes?

NORA: If your little squirrel asked you for something, and she was very, very nice . . .

TORVALD: What?

NORA: Would you do it?

TORVALD: I'd want to hear what it was first.

NORA: Your little squirrel would run all over the place and do her little tricks. You just have to be nice and do what she wants.

TORVALD: Tell me what you mean.

NORA: Your skylark would sing, warble in every room, singing loud, singing soft . . .

TORVALD: Well, she does that anyway.

NORA: I'd be a fairy and dance for you in the moonlight, Torvald.

TORVALD: Nora, you're not talking about—the thing you asked of me this morning. . . .

NORA: *(going toward him)* Yes, Torvald. I beg you, I beg you.

TORVALD: How dare you bring up that business again?

NORA: You *must* do as I ask. You *must* let Krogstad keep his job at the bank.

TORVALD: My dear Nora, I have arranged to give his position to Mrs. Linde.

NORA: Yes, I know you've been really kind about that. But you could just as easily fire someone other than Krogstad.

TORVALD: You are being *incredibly* stubborn. Just because you chose to give him so thoughtless a promise—that you would speak on his behalf— I'm supposed to—

NORA: That's not the reason, Torvald. I'm doing this for you. This man writes for the most dreadful, slanderous newspapers. You told me so yourself. He can do you a terrible amount of harm. I'm scared to death of him—

TORVALD: Oh, I understand. You're thinking about the past and you're afraid.

61

NORA: What do you mean?

TORVALD: Well, of course you're thinking about your father.

NORA: Yes. Yes, that's it. Just remember what those malicious people wrote in the papers about Papa, how they slandered him. I'm sure they would have had him dismissed if the Department had not sent you over to look into the matter, and if you hadn't been so kind and helpful to him.

TORVALD: My dear Nora. There's a very important difference between your father and me. Your father's reputation as a public official was not above suspicion. Mine *is*—and I hope it will remain so, as long as I hold my position.

NORA: But you can never tell what these people might do to you! We ought to have enough money to be comfortable, we ought to be cozy and happy in our quiet little home. We should have no cares. You and I and the children. That is why I'm begging you.

TORVALD: And it's just because you *are* pleading on his behalf that you make it impossible for me to keep him on. Everyone at the bank already knows that I intend to dismiss Krogstad. Are people going to say now that the new manager has changed his mind just because his wife asked him?

NORA: And what if they did?

TORVALD: Oh yes. Just so this stubborn little woman can get her own way. Do you think I'm going to make myself look like a fool in front of my whole staff? Do you think I'm going to let people think I'm a man who will change his mind because of outside pressures? I can assure you I'd feel the consequences of that pretty quickly. And in any case, there's one thing that makes it impossible for me to keep Krogstad at the bank as long as I am the manager.

NORA: What's that?

TORVALD: I might perhaps have overlooked his moral failings if I had to—

NORA: Yes, you could, couldn't you?

TORVALD: —and I hear that he's a hard worker. *But* I knew him when we were boys. It was one of those impulsive friendships that often haunt one in later life. I might as well tell you quite plainly that we were once on very intimate terms with one another. But this man has no tact when other people are around. On the contrary, he thinks our past friendship gives him the right to be on familiar terms with me. All the time it's "Hi there, Torvald, old pal!" That sort of thing. It is *extremely* difficult for me. He would make my position in the bank totally intolerable.

NORA: Torvald, I can't believe you mean that.

TORVALD: Can't you? Why not?

NORA: Because it's such a narrow-minded way of looking at things.

TORVALD: Narrow-minded? What do you mean? Do you think I'm narrow-minded?

NORA: No, just the opposite, my love. And that is why . . .

TORVALD: No. You said that I had a narrow-minded way of looking at things. Well then, *I* myself must be narrow-minded. All right, I'm going to put an end to this. *(he goes to the hall door and calls out)* Helene!

NORA: What are you going to do?

TORVALD: *(rummaging through his papers)* Settle it once and for all. *(Maid enters)* Here. Take this letter, go downstairs, and find a messenger. Immediately. Tell him to deliver it right away. The address is on it. Here's the money.

MAID: Yes, sir. *(exits with the letter)*

TORVALD: *(putting his papers together)* Now then, Madam Stubborn.

NORA: *(almost out of breath)* Torvald, what was that letter?

TORVALD: Krogstad's dismissal.

NORA: Call her back, Torvald. There's still time. Torvald, call her back! Do it for me, do it for you, do it for the children. Do you hear me, Torvald, call her back! You don't know what this letter can do to us.

TORVALD: It's too late.

NORA: Yes, it's too late.

TORVALD: My dear Nora. I can forgive you for being so upset. But it really is an insult to me. Isn't it an insult to think that I should be afraid of a starving pen pusher? But I forgive you because, in its own way, it speaks so eloquently of your love for me. *(he takes her in his arms)* And that is how it should be, my darling Nora. You can be sure that whatever happens, I will be brave and strong. You'll see that I am man enough to take everything upon myself.

64

NORA: *(her voice is horror-stricken)* What do you mean by that?

TORVALD: Everything . . .

NORA: *(recovering)* You'll never have to do that.

TORVALD: Well, well, we'll share the burden, Nora, as man and wife should. That's how it's going to be. *(putting his arms around her)* Are you happy now? There, there. No more frightened little dove's eyes. It's all in your imagination. So. You must go and rehearse the tarantella and practice on the tambourine. I'll go into the office and shut the door, and I will hear nothing. You can make as much noise as you like. *(turns back at the door)* And when Dr. Rank comes, tell him where he can find me. *(nods to her, takes his papers, goes into his room, and shuts the door)*

NORA: *(Nora is rooted to the spot, very bewildered, and whispers to herself)* He actually could do it. He *will* do it. He'll do it in spite of everything. No, no, no. Never, never. Anything rather than that. I need help . . . anything. *(the doorbell rings in a familiar pattern)* Dr. Rank! Anything! Anything other than that . . . *(She puts her hands over her face, pulls herself together, opens the door. Rank is standing in the hall, hanging up his coat. During the following conversation, it begins to grow dark.)*

NORA: Good day, Dr. Rank. I recognized your ring. But you mustn't go in to Torvald now. I think he's busy.

DR. RANK: And you?

NORA: *(ushers him in and shuts the door)* Oh, you know that I always have time for you.

DR. RANK: Thank you. I shall take advantage of that for as long as I can.

NORA: What do you mean by that? For as long as you can?

DR. RANK: Does that alarm you?

NORA: It was such a strange way of putting it. Is something going to happen?

DR. RANK: Nothing that I haven't been preparing for. But I didn't expect it to happen so soon.

NORA: *(holding him tightly by the arm)* What did they tell you? Dr. Rank, you must talk to me.

DR. RANK: *(sitting down by the stove)* It's all over. Nothing can be done.

NORA: *(with a sigh of relief)* Are you talking about yourself?

DR. RANK: Who else? You can't lie to yourself. I'm the worst of all my patients, Mrs. Helmer. Recently I've been assessing my internal net worth. And I'm bankrupt. Perhaps within a month I'll lie rotting in the graveyard.

NORA: What a disgusting thing to say!

DR. RANK: Well, it *is* disgusting. And the fact is that I will have to endure so much more before the graveyard. I will make only one more examination of myself. When I've done that I will know— with some certainty—when the disintegration will begin. There's something I want to tell you. Torvald . . . is a very refined man. That makes him absolutely incapable of facing anything that is unpleasant. I won't have him visit me in my sickroom.

66

NORA: Oh but Dr. Rank . . .

DR. RANK: I won't have him in there. Not under any circumstances. My door is locked to him. As soon as I am absolutely sure that the end is coming, I will send you my card with a black cross on it. And then you will know that the pain and suffering is coming to an end.

NORA: You are talking nonsense. I wanted you to be so happy today.

DR. RANK: With death watching my every move? To have to suffer this because of another man's sin. There's no justice. In every single family, in one way or another, there is some inexorable curse which brings retribution.

NORA: *(putting her hands over her ears)* Nonsense. Talk about something happy!

DR. RANK: Oh, we can laugh about the whole thing! My innocent spine has to suffer because my father, well, enjoyed himself when he was young.

NORA: *(sitting at the table on the left)* You mean that he loved asparagus and pâté de foie gras and that sort of thing, don't you?

DR. RANK: Yes, and truffles.

NORA: Yes, truffles. And oysters too, I'm sure.

DR. RANK: Oysters, yes of course.

NORA: And gallons of port and champagne. It's so sad that all these wonderful things should attack our bodies.

DR. RANK: Especially sad that they should take revenge on the bodies of those who didn't have the chance to enjoy them.

NORA: Yes. That's the worst part.

DR. RANK: *(looking at her carefully)* Hmm.

NORA: *(after a short pause)* Why did you smile?

DR. RANK: No, it was you.

NORA: No, it was you, Dr. Rank.

DR. RANK: *(getting up)* You're a much greater tease than I thought.

NORA: Well, I'm in a silly mood today.

DR. RANK: So it seems.

NORA: *(putting her hands on his shoulders)* Dear, dear, Dr. Rank. Death cannot ever take you away from Torvald and me.

DR. RANK: Oh, you'd easily recover from the loss. The departed are soon forgotten.

NORA: *(looking at him anxiously)* Do you believe that?

DR. RANK: People form new friendships.

NORA: Who will form new friendships?

DR. RANK: You and Torvald, when I'm gone. You're already well on the way, I think. What did Mrs. Linde want here last night?

NORA: Aha! You don't mean to say that you're jealous of Kristine?

DR. RANK: Yes, I am. She will take over from me in this house. When I'm gone this woman will—

NORA: Shh! Keep your voice down. She's in the other room.

DR. RANK: Today again. You see?

68

NORA: She's only come to sew my dress for me. Good heavens, you're totally unreasonable. *(sitting down on the sofa)* Now be nice, Dr. Rank. And tomorrow you'll see how beautifully I shall dance. And you can think that I'm dancing all for you— and for Torvald too, of course. *(taking various things out of the box)* Dr. Rank, come and sit down over here. I want to show you something.

DR. RANK: *(sitting down)* What is it?

NORA: Just look at these.

DR. RANK: Silk stockings.

NORA: Flesh-colored. Aren't they beautiful? It's so dark in here now, but tomorrow—no, no, no! You must only look at the feet! Oh well. You can have a little look at the legs too.

DR. RANK: Hmm.

NORA: Why do you look so doubtful? Don't you think they'll fit me?

DR. RANK: I have no way of forming an opinion on that.

NORA: *(looking at him for a moment)* Shame on you! *(hitting him lightly on the ear with the stockings)* That's to punish you. *(folding them up again)*

DR. RANK: And what other nice little things am I going to be allowed to see?

NORA: Not a thing more. Nothing. You were so naughty. *(she looks among the things humming to herself)*

DR. RANK: *(after a short silence)* When I'm sitting here, talking to you, so intimately, I can't imagine—

even for a second—what would have happened to me if I'd never come into this house.

NORA: *(smiling)* I think you really do feel at home with us.

DR. RANK: *(in a low voice, looking straight ahead)* And to have to leave it all.

NORA: Nonsense. You're not going to leave it all.

DR. RANK: *(recovering)* And not to be able to leave behind even the slightest token of one's thanks, not even a fleeting regret—nothing but an empty place which the first person who comes will fill as well as anyone else.

NORA: And if I asked you now for a— no . . .

DR. RANK: For what?

NORA: For something that really proves the depth of your friendship.

DR. RANK: Yes, yes.

NORA: I mean a really big favor.

DR. RANK: Would you honestly make me so happy, just for once?

NORA: But you don't know what it is yet.

DR. RANK: No, but tell me.

NORA: I really can't, Dr. Rank. It's something that makes no sense. I need advice, I need help, I need a favor.

DR. RANK: The bigger it is, the better. I've no idea what you mean. Tell me. Can't you trust me?

NORA: More than anyone else. I know you are my best, my truest friend. So I will tell you what it is.

Dr. Rank, it is something you must help me stop from happening. You know how much Torvald loves me, how devoted he is, how inexpressibly deep his love for me is. He'd never, even for a second, hesitate to give his life for me.

DR. RANK: *(leaning toward her)* Nora—do you think he's the only one? . . .

NORA: *(with a slight start)* The only one?

DR. RANK: The only one who would give his life for you. . . .

NORA: *(sadly)* Ah. Is that it?

DR. RANK: I was determined that you should know that before I . . . went away. There will never be a better opportunity than now. So now you know, Nora. And now you know too that you can trust me in a way that you couldn't trust anyone else.

NORA: *(rising deliberately and quietly)* Let me get by you.

DR. RANK: *(making room for her to pass by but sitting still)* Nora.

NORA: *(at the hall door)* Helene! Bring in the lamp! *(going over to the stove)* Dear Dr. Rank, that was really awful of you.

DR. RANK: To have loved you as much as everybody else? Was that awful?

NORA: No. But to *tell* me! There was really no need.

DR. RANK: What do you mean? Did you know? *(Maid enters with lamp, sets it down on the table, and exits)* Nora—Mrs. Helmer—tell me, did you have any idea of this?

NORA: Oh, how would I know whether I had any idea or not? I really can't tell you. But for you to be so clumsy, Dr. Rank! We were getting on so well.

DR. RANK: In any case, now you know that you can have your way with me, body and soul. So, won't you tell me what's on your mind?

NORA: *(looking at him)* After what just happened?

DR. RANK: I beg you. Tell me what it is.

NORA: I can't tell you anything now.

DR. RANK: No, no, you mustn't punish me like that. Let me do for you whatever a man can do.

NORA: You can do nothing for me now. Anyway, I really don't need any help. You'll find that the whole thing is just . . . my imagination. It really is! Of course it is! *(sitting down in the rocking chair and smiling)* You're really a terrible man, aren't you, Dr. Rank? Aren't you ashamed of yourself now that the light is on?

DR. RANK: Not at all. But perhaps I had better go— go for good.

NORA: No you will not. You must come here every day, just as before. You know very well that Torvald needs you.

DR. RANK: Yes. And you?

NORA: Oh, I'm always wonderfully happy when you come.

DR. RANK: That's exactly what confused me. You are an enigma to me. I have often thought that you would just as soon share my company as Torvald's.

72

NORA: Yes, you see there are those whom one loves and those whom one would choose to spend one's time with.

DR. RANK: There's something in that.

NORA: When I was at home I loved Papa most of all. But I always had great fun sneaking off to the maids' quarters. They never passed judgment, and they always talked to each other about such amusing things.

DR. RANK: Oh, I see—I've taken *their* place.

NORA: (*jumping up and going to him*) Oh dear, sweet Dr. Rank. That's not what I meant at all. But I'm sure you understand that being with Torvald is a little bit like being with Papa. . . .

(*Maid enters from the hallway*)

MAID: Excuse me, ma'am. (*whispers and hands her a card*)

NORA: (*glancing at card*) Oh! (*puts card in her pocket*)

DR. RANK: Is anything the matter?

NORA: No, no, nothing at all. It's just . . . just . . . it's my new dress. . . .

DR. RANK: But your dress is over there.

NORA: Oh yes, that one. This is a new one. I ordered it. Torvald mustn't find out about it—

DR. RANK: So that was your great secret!

NORA: Of course, of course. Just go in to him. He's sitting in the inner room. Keep him there as long as you—

DR. RANK: You can rest assured I won't let him get away. (*goes into Torvald's study*)

73

NORA: *(to Maid)* He's waiting in the kitchen?

MAID: Yes, he came up the back stairs.

NORA: Didn't you tell him no one was home?

MAID: Yes. But that didn't do any good.

NORA: He won't go away?

MAID: No. He says he won't go till he sees you, ma'am.

NORA: Well, let him come in. But quietly! Helene, you mustn't say a word about this to anybody. It's a surprise—for my husband.

MAID: Yes, ma'am. I understand. *(exit)*

NORA: It's going to happen! This terrible, terrible thing. I can't do anything to stop it. No, no, no, it can't happen. It will not happen. *(She bolts the door of the study. The Maid opens the hall door for Krogstad and then closes it. He is wearing a fur coat and hat and high boots.)*

NORA: *(going toward him)* Keep your voice down—my husband is at home.

KROGSTAD: It doesn't matter about that.

NORA: What do you want from me?

KROGSTAD: I want you to explain something.

NORA: Hurry up, then. What is it?

KROGSTAD: I'm sure you know that I have been dismissed.

NORA: There was nothing I could do, Mr. Krogstad. I tried to interfere, I really, really did, but it was no use.

74

KROGSTAD: Does your husband have so little love for you? He knows what damage I can do to you, and yet he persists—

NORA: How could you think that he knows anything about this?

KROGSTAD: No. I suppose not. It would not be at all like our respected Torvald Helmer to have the courage—

NORA: Please, Mr. Krogstad, show my husband some respect.

KROGSTAD: All the respect he deserves. So. You've kept all this business to yourself. Then I guess you've got a clearer picture than you had yesterday of what it is that you have done.

NORA: More than you could ever show me.

KROGSTAD: Yes, I'm such a "poor lawyer."

NORA: What do you want from me?

KROGSTAD: I only wanted to see how you were, Mrs. Helmer. I've been thinking about you all day. I'm just a clerk, a pen-pusher, a—well, even a man like me has some feelings, you know.

NORA: Then why don't you show them? Think of my little children.

KROGSTAD: Did you or your husband ever think of mine? Never mind about that. I came to tell you that you mustn't worry too much. First of all, I am not going to bring any formal charges.

NORA: No, of course, I was sure you wouldn't.

KROGSTAD: The whole thing can be settled quite amicably. There's no reason why anyone should know anything about it. We'll keep it a secret between the three of us.

NORA: My husband must never find out anything about it.

KROGSTAD: And how will you stop that? Are you saying that you can pay off the balance?

NORA: No, not just at the moment.

KROGSTAD: Perhaps you have a plan for raising the money fairly soon?

NORA: No plan that I would put into practice.

KROGSTAD: Well, in any case it wouldn't have been any use. If you stood there with your hands full of money, I still wouldn't give you back the contract.

NORA: And what do you intend doing with it?

KROGSTAD: Nothing. I shall just hold on to it—keep it in my possession. No one who's not involved need know anything about it. So if you've been thinking of doing something desperate—

NORA: I have.

KROGSTAD: If you've been thinking of running away from home—

NORA: I have.

KROGSTAD: —or even worse—

NORA: How did you know?

KROGSTAD: —then give up the idea.

NORA: How did you know I had thought of *that*?

KROGSTAD: Most of us think of that at first. I did too. But I didn't have the courage.

76

NORA: *(faintly)* Neither did I.

KROGSTAD: *(sounding relieved)* No. That's it, isn't it? You didn't have the courage.

NORA: No. I haven't, I haven't.

KROGSTAD: Besides, it would have been a very foolish thing to do. Once the first domestic storm has passed—. Well, I have a letter for your husband in my pocket.

NORA: Telling him everything?

KROGSTAD: As gently as possible.

NORA: *(quickly)* He mustn't get that letter. Tear it up. I'll get some money somehow.

KROGSTAD: But Mrs. Helmer, I think I told you just now—

NORA: I'm not talking about the money I owe you. Just tell me how much you're asking my husband for, and I'll get it for you.

KROGSTAD: I'm not asking your husband for a penny.

NORA: What do you want then?

KROGSTAD: Listen. I want to get my reputation back, Mrs. Helmer. And your husband is going to have to help me. For the past year and a half my life has been exemplary—even though it was a struggle and I had very little money. I was happy to make my way up step by step. But now I've been thrown back down again. And it's not going to be enough for me just to be taken back in again. I tell you—I want to get ahead. I want to get back into the bank but in a better job. Your husband must find a place for me—

NORA: He will never do that.

77

KROGSTAD: Oh yes he will. I know him. He won't utter a peep. And as soon as I'm back in there again, with him, you'll see! Within a year I'll be the manager's right-hand man. It'll be Nils Krogstad, not Torvald Helmer, who's running the bank.

NORA: You'll never see the day. . . .

KROGSTAD: Do you mean that you will—?

NORA: Now I have the courage.

KROGSTAD: You don't frighten me. A fine, pampered lady like you—

NORA: You'll see, you'll see.

KROGSTAD: Under the ice, perhaps? Down, down into the black, icy water. And then in the spring you'll float up to the surface all bloated and unrecognizable, your hair fallen out.

NORA: You don't frighten me.

KROGSTAD: Nor you me. Mrs. Helmer, people don't do such things. In any case, what would be the use? He would still be completely in my power.

NORA: Even then? When I am no longer—

KROGSTAD: Don't forget that I am in complete control of your reputation. *(Nora is speechless and just stares at him)* So. Now I have warned you. Don't do anything foolish. When Torvald has gotten my letter, I expect a reply from him. And don't you forget that it is your husband who has forced me to do this sort of thing again. I can never forgive him for that. Goodbye, Mrs. Helmer. *(exits through the hall)*

NORA: *(goes to the hall door, opens it slightly, and listens)* He's going. He's not putting the letter in the box. No. No. It couldn't happen! *(opens the door slowly)* What? He's standing outside and not going downstairs. Did he change his mind? Is he . . . ? *(The letter is dropped in the box, and Krogstad's footsteps can be heard going down the stairs. Nora stifles a cry, then runs across the room to the table by the sofa. A short pause.)* It's in the mailbox. *(crosses back to the door)* There it is. Oh Torvald, Torvald, there's no hope for us now!

(Mrs. Linde comes in from the room on the left with the dress)

MRS. LINDE: There. I think it's all done. Would you like to try it on—?

NORA: *(in a hoarse whisper)* Kristine, come here.

MRS. LINDE: *(throwing the dress down on the sofa)* What's the matter? You look so upset!

NORA: Come here. Do you see that letter? There, look—you can see it through the glass in the mailbox.

MRS. LINDE: Yes, I can see it.

NORA: That letter is from Krogstad.

MRS. LINDE: Nora—Krogstad lent you the money!

NORA: Yes. And now Torvald will find out all about it.

MRS. LINDE: Believe me, Nora, that's the best thing that could happen—for both of you.

NORA: But there's something you don't know—I forged a signature.

MRS. LINDE: Good heavens—!

NORA: I'm telling this only to you, Kristine. I want you to be my witness.

MRS. LINDE: Your witness? What do you mean? What do you want me to—?

NORA: If I should lose my mind—no, it could easily happen—

MRS. LINDE: Nora!

NORA: Or if anything else should happen to me—anything . . . and I weren't to be here . . .

MRS. LINDE: Nora! Nora, you're out of your mind.

NORA: And if it turned out that someone wanted to take all the responsibility, all the blame . . . you understand? . . .

MRS. LINDE: Yes. Yes. But how could you think . . . ?

NORA: You must be my witness that *it is not true*. Kristine, I am not out of my mind. In fact I have come to my senses. And I repeat: no one else knows anything about this. I and I alone did it. Remember that.

MRS. LINDE: I promise you I will. But I don't understand all of this.

NORA: How could you? A miracle is about to happen. . . .

MRS. LINDE: A miracle?

NORA: Yes. A miracle. But it's so devastating, Kristine. It mustn't happen—not for all the world.

MRS. LINDE: I will go and see Krogstad right away.

NORA: No. You mustn't. He might do you some harm.

MRS. LINDE: There was a time when he would have done anything for me.

NORA: Krogstad?

MRS. LINDE: Where does he live?

NORA: How would I know? Oh yes— *(feeling in her pocket)* here's his card. But the letter, the letter—!

TORVALD: *(calling from his room, knocking on the door)* Nora!

NORA: *(anxiously)* What is it? What do you want?

TORVALD: Don't be alarmed. We're not coming in. You've locked the door. Are you trying on your dress?

NORA: Yes, I am. I look so nice, Torvald.

MRS. LINDE: *(she has read the card)* He lives just round the corner.

NORA: But it's no use. It's hopeless. The letter is lying there in the box.

MRS. LINDE: And your husband has the key?

NORA: Yes. He always has it.

MRS. LINDE: Krogstad must ask for his letter back before your husband reads it. He must make up some excuse.

NORA: But Torvald always at this time of day—

MRS. LINDE: Find some way of stopping him. Go in and see him while I'm gone. I'll be back as soon as I can. *(she goes out quickly)*

81

NORA: *(goes to Torvald's door, opens it, and peeps in)* Torvald!

TORVALD: *(from inside)* Well? Am I finally allowed into my own room? Come along, Rank, now you're going to see— *(stopping in the doorway)* What's this?

NORA: What's what, dear?

TORVALD: Rank had led me to believe there would be a wonderful transformation.

DR. RANK: *(in doorway)* That's what I thought. But evidently I was wrong.

NORA: Well, no one can admire me in my dress until tomorrow night.

TORVALD: My dear Nora, you look exhausted. Have you been doing too much rehearsing?

NORA: No. I've not rehearsed at all.

TORVALD: But you'll have to . . .

NORA: Yes, Torvald, I know I do. But I can't make any progress at all without you. I've totally forgotten the whole thing.

TORVALD: Oh, we'll soon get it right again.

NORA: Yes, help me Torvald. Promise me. I'm so nervous about it. All those people. . . . You must give me all your time this evening. No more business—you mustn't even pick up a pen. Promise me, Torvald dear.

TORVALD: I promise. This evening I will be totally at your service, you helpless little creature. Oh, but while I think of it, I'll just go and— *(goes toward the hall door)*

NORA: Where are you going?

TORVALD: To see if there's any mail.

NORA: No. No, don't do that, Torvald.

TORVALD: Why not?

NORA: Torvald, please don't. There's nothing there.

TORVALD: Well, let me look. *(Turns to go to the mailbox. Nora goes to the piano and plays the first bars of the tarantella. Torvald stops in the doorway.)* Aha!

NORA: I can't dance tomorrow if I don't rehearse.

TORVALD: *(going to her)* Are you really so nervous about it?

NORA: Yes, I really am. Let me rehearse right now. There's time before we go to dinner. Sit down and play for me, Torvald. You can make criticisms and correct me if I do the wrong steps.

TORVALD: Well, if you want me to—with pleasure! *(sits at piano)*

NORA: *(Takes a tambourine out of the box along with a long, brightly colored shawl, which she drapes around her shoulders. She leaps to the front of the room and calls out.)* Now play for me. I'm going to dance.

(Torvald plays and Nora dances. Dr. Rank stands behind Torvald at the piano and watches.)

TORVALD: *(playing)* Slower! Slower!

NORA: This is the only way I know how!

TORVALD: Not so violently, Nora!

NORA: No, this is right!

TORVALD: *(stopping playing)* No. No. That's all wrong.

NORA: Didn't I tell you?

DR. RANK: Let me play for her.

TORVALD: *(getting up)* Yes, do. It'll be easier for me to correct her.

(Dr. Rank sits down and plays. Nora dances more and more wildly. Torvald is standing by the stove and gives her frequent instructions. She seems oblivious. Her hair falls down over her shoulders. She pays no attention to it and goes on dancing. Enter Mrs. Linde.)

MRS. LINDE: *(standing in awe at the door)* Oh!!

NORA: *(dancing)* It's such fun, Kristine.

TORVALD: Nora, my darling, you're dancing as if your life depended on it.

NORA: It does, it does.

TORVALD: Stop, Rank, stop! This is sheer madness. Stop, I tell you. *(Dr. Rank stops playing. Nora suddenly stands still. Torvald goes up to her.)* I would never have believed it. You've forgotten everything I taught you.

NORA: *(tossing aside the tambourine)* There you are, you see?

TORVALD: You need a lot of coaching.

NORA: Yes, I really do. You must teach me right up to the last minute. Promise me, Torvald!

TORVALD: You can depend on me.

NORA: You must think only of me—nothing else. Not today or tomorrow. You mustn't open a single letter, not even go near the mailbox—

TORVALD: So, you're still afraid of that man—

NORA: Yes, I am.

TORVALD: Nora, I can tell by your face that there's a letter from him out there.

NORA: I don't know. Perhaps there is. But you mustn't read anything like that right now. We mustn't let anything dreadful come between us until this is all over.

DR. RANK: *(whispers to Torvald)* You mustn't contradict her.

TORVALD: *(taking her in his arms)* My little one shall have her own way. But tomorrow night, after you've danced—

NORA: You will be free—

(the Maid appears in the doorway on the right)

MAID: Dinner is served, ma'am.

NORA: We will have champagne, Helene.

MAID: Very good, ma'am.

TORVALD: Well, well, well—we're having a banquet!

NORA: Yes. A champagne banquet till the wee small hours. *(calling out)* And—Helene—some macaroons! Lots. Just for once!

TORVALD: Calm down! Don't be so nervous! Be my own little lark, as always.

NORA: Yes, dear, I will. But go in now. You too, Dr. Rank. Kristine, would you help me put my hair up?

DR. RANK: *(whispering to Torvald as they go out)* There isn't anything, um . . . She's not expecting . . . ?

TORVALD: Oh no, nothing like that. . . . It's just another instance of this childlike nervousness I was telling you about. *(they exit to the right)*

NORA: Well?

MRS. LINDE: Gone out of town.

NORA: I could tell from your face.

MRS. LINDE: He's coming back tomorrow evening. I left him a note.

NORA: You shouldn't have done anything. You must let everything take its course. In a way, it's wonderful to be waiting for a miracle.

MRS. LINDE: And what are you waiting for?

NORA: Oh, you wouldn't understand. Go in and join them. I'll be in in a moment. (*Mrs. Linde goes into the dining room. Nora stands still for a while, as if regaining her composure. Then she looks at her watch.*) Five o'clock. Seven hours till midnight. Then twenty-four hours till the next midnight. Then the tarantella will be finished. Twenty-four plus seven? Thirty-one hours to live.

TORVALD: (*from the doorway*) Where's my little lark?

NORA: (*going to him with her arms outstretched*) Here she is!

ACT 3

The same setting. The table has been placed in the center of the room, with chairs around it. A lamp is on the table. The hallway door is open. Music is heard from upstairs. Mrs. Linde is sitting at the table, slowly turning the pages of a book. She tries to concentrate but cannot. Every now and then she listens for a sound from the hallway.

MRS. LINDE: He's not here yet . . . *(looking at her watch)* . . . and the time is nearly up. If he doesn't— *(Goes to the outer hall and opens the downstairs door carefully. Quiet footsteps are heard on the stairs. She whispers.)* Come in. There's no one here.

KROGSTAD: *(in the doorway)* I got the note from you at home. What is this all about?

MRS. LINDE: *I have* to talk to you.

KROGSTAD: Really? And do *I have* to be *here*?

MRS. LINDE: Look, I couldn't possibly meet with you where I live. There's no private entrance to my rooms. Come in. We are quite alone. The maid is asleep, and the Helmers are at the party upstairs.

KROGSTAD: Are the Helmers really going to a party tonight?

MRS. LINDE: Yes. Why not?

KROGSTAD: Of course, why not?

MRS. LINDE: Now, Nils, we must have a talk.

87

KROGSTAD: What can we two possibly have to talk about?

MRS. LINDE: A great deal, I think.

KROGSTAD: I wouldn't have thought so.

MRS. LINDE: No. I don't think you ever really understood me.

KROGSTAD: What was there to understand? The whole world saw exactly what was happening—a woman without any feelings was leaving her man when a more lucrative prospect showed up.

MRS. LINDE: Do you really believe that I have no feelings? And do you think it was so easy for me to do it?

KROGSTAD: Wasn't it?

MRS. LINDE: Nils, did you really think so?

KROGSTAD: If your version of events is right, then why did you write me that letter?

MRS. LINDE: What else could I do? I *had* to break up with you. And so it was my duty to kill any feelings you had for me.

KROGSTAD: *(flexing his hands)* So that was it. All that— all for money.

MRS. LINDE: Remember that I had an invalid mother and two little brothers to take care of. We couldn't wait for you, Nils. You didn't have any prospects at the time.

KROGSTAD: That may be true. But you had no right to leave me for another man.

MRS. LINDE: I don't know, I don't know. I've asked myself many times if I had that right.

KROGSTAD: *(in a gentler tone)* When I lost you, I felt as if the ground beneath my feet had given way. Look at me now—I'm like a shipwrecked man clinging to a piece of wreckage.

MRS. LINDE: But help may be near.

KROGSTAD: It *was* near. But then you came and got in my way.

MRS. LINDE: I didn't intend to, Nils. I only found out today that I was going to take your place at the bank.

KROGSTAD: If you say so, I believe you. But now that you know, aren't you going to let me keep it?

MRS. LINDE: No, because there would be no benefit for you at all.

KROGSTAD: "Benefit, benefit!"—that's what *I* would do.

MRS. LINDE: I have learned to think carefully before I act. Life and bitter necessity have taught me that.

KROGSTAD: And life has taught me not to trust fine speeches.

MRS. LINDE: Then life has taught you something very useful. But surely you must believe in actions?

KROGSTAD: What do you mean?

MRS. LINDE: You said you were like a shipwrecked man clinging to a piece of wreckage.

KROGSTAD: I had every reason to say that.

MRS. LINDE: Well, I'm like a shipwrecked woman clinging to a piece of wreckage—no one to mourn for, to care for.

KROGSTAD: You made that choice.

MRS. LINDE: At that time there was no other choice.

KROGSTAD: Well, what about now?

MRS. LINDE: Nils, what would you think of us two shipwrecked people joining together?

KROGSTAD: What do you mean?

MRS. LINDE: Two people on the same piece of wreckage would stand a better chance than on their own.

KROGSTAD: Kristine!

MRS. LINDE: Why do you think I came to town?

KROGSTAD: You mean that you were thinking of me?

MRS. LINDE: I couldn't bear to live without working. All my life, for as long as I can remember, I have worked. It has been my greatest, my only pleasure. But now I'm all alone in the world. My life is empty, and I feel lost. There is no pleasure at all in working for oneself. Nils, give me something, give me someone to work for.

KROGSTAD: How can I trust that? It's just a woman's overly exaggerated sense of decency that makes you suggest that.

MRS. LINDE: Have you ever noticed such a thing in me before?

KROGSTAD: Could you really do this? You know all about my past?

MRS. LINDE: Yes.

KROGSTAD: And you know my reputation in this town?

MRS. LINDE: Just now you seemed to imply that if you'd been with me, you might have been a different man.

KROGSTAD: I'm sure of it.

MRS. LINDE: Is it too late?

KROGSTAD: Have you thought about this carefully, Kristine? Yes, I'm sure you have. I can see it in your face. Do you really have the courage—?

MRS. LINDE: I want to be a mother to someone. Your children need a mother. And we two need each other. Nils, I have faith in the real you—I can face anything with you.

KROGSTAD: *(taking her hands)* Thank you, thank you, Kristine. Now I must find a way to regain my reputation in the world. Oh, but I forgot—

MRS. LINDE: *(listening)* Sh! The tarantella! Go, go now.

KROGSTAD: Why? What is it?

MRS. LINDE: Can't you hear them upstairs? When the dance is over, they'll be downstairs immediately.

KROGSTAD: Yes, I'll go. But none of this is any use. I'm sure you don't know what steps I've taken as regards the Helmers.

MRS. LINDE: Yes, I know all about that.

KROGSTAD: And you still can—?

MRS. LINDE: I can understand to what lengths a man like you might go when you have no hope.

KROGSTAD: If only I could undo what I have done.

MRS. LINDE: You can't. Your letter is out there in the mailbox.

KROGSTAD: Are you sure?

MRS. LINDE: Quite sure, but—

KROGSTAD: *(looking at her carefully)* Is that what all this is about? You want to save your friend no matter the cost? Tell me . . . tell me honestly, is that it?

MRS. LINDE: Nils, a woman who has sold out once before to help someone else doesn't do it a second time.

KROGSTAD: I'll ask for my letter back.

MRS. LINDE: No.

KROGSTAD: Yes, of course I will. I'll wait here until Torvald comes down. I'll tell him he must give me my letter back—that it's only about my dismissal—that he mustn't read it.

MRS. LINDE: No, Nils, you mustn't ask for your letter back.

KROGSTAD: Tell me the truth. Isn't that why you asked me to meet you here?

MRS. LINDE: At first, yes. I was frightened. But twenty-four hours have passed since then, and in that time I have observed some incredible things happening in this house. Torvald must find out all about it. This painful secret must be revealed. They must come to a complete understanding between themselves. That is impossible with all this deception, this hiding of the truth.

KROGSTAD: All right. As long as you take full responsibility. But there is one thing I can do. And I will do it at once.

MRS. LINDE: *(listening)* You must go quickly. The dance is over, it's not safe for us here any longer.

KROGSTAD: I will wait for you down below.

MRS. LINDE: Yes, wait for me. You'll walk me home.

KROGSTAD: I've never had such an amazing piece of luck in my life. *(he goes out through the outer door, but the door between the living room and the hall remains open)*

MRS. LINDE: *(tidying up the room and getting her hat and cloak ready)* What a difference, what a difference! Someone to work for, someone to live for—a home to take care of. And I will do that. I wish they'd hurry up and come— *(listens)* There they are now. I'd better put on my things. *(takes up her hat and cloak)*

(Torvald and Nora can be heard talking outside. A key is turned. Torvald brings Nora almost forcibly into the hall. She is wearing her Italian costume and a large black shawl. Torvald is in evening dress with a black cloak open over his shoulders.)

NORA: *(struggling with Torvald in the doorway)* No, no, don't make me go in. I want to go back upstairs. I don't want to leave so early.

TORVALD: But my dearest Nora . . .

NORA: Please, Torvald dear, *please*—just for an hour longer.

TORVALD: Not for a minute, my sweet Nora. You know that's what we agreed. Come in here. You'll catch a cold out there. *(he brings her gently into the room even though she resists)*

MRS. LINDE: Good evening.

NORA: Kristine!

TORVALD: You're here so late, Mrs. Linde?

MRS. LINDE: Yes. Please excuse me. I really wanted to see Nora in her dress.

93

NORA: And you've been sitting here waiting for me?

MRS. LINDE: Yes. Unfortunately, I came too late, you'd already gone upstairs. And I thought to myself that I couldn't leave without seeing you.

TORVALD: *(taking off Nora's shawl)* Well? Have a good look at her. I think she's worth a look. Isn't she beautiful, Mrs. Linde?

MRS. LINDE: Yes, she really is.

TORVALD: Doesn't she look remarkably lovely? Everyone thought so at the ball. But this sweet little thing is terribly stubborn. What are we going to do with her? It's hard to believe, but I almost had to drag her away.

NORA: Torvald, you will be very sorry for not letting me stay, even for just half an hour.

TORVALD: Listen to her, Mrs. Linde! She danced the tarantella. She was an enormous success, and she deserved it. Although perhaps the performance was somewhat too realistic—a little more . . . I mean . . . than artistic conventions demanded. But never mind. The important thing is, she was a success. She was an enormous success. Do you think I'd let her stay after that, and spoil the effect? No indeed. I put my arm around the lovely little girl from Capri—my *Capri*cious little girl from Capri, I should say. We made one round of the room, we bowed to either side, and, as they say in romantic novels, the beautiful vision disappeared. An exit always ought to be perfectly timed, Mrs. Linde. But I can't make Nora understand that! Phew! This room is hot. *(throws his cloak on a chair and opens the door of his study)* Oh! It's all dark in here. Oh, of course—excuse me— *(he goes in and lights some candles)*

94

NORA: *(quickly and in a whisper)* Well?

MRS. LINDE: *(in a low voice)* I've talked with him.

NORA: Yes, and?

MRS. LINDE: Nora, you've got to tell your husband all about it.

NORA: *(without any expression)* I knew it.

MRS. LINDE: You have nothing to be afraid of from Krogstad. But you must tell your husband.

NORA: I won't tell him.

MRS. LINDE: Then the letter will.

NORA: Thank you, Kristine. Now I know what I have to do. Sh!

TORVALD: *(coming in)* Well, Mrs. Linde, have you admired her?

MRS. LINDE: Yes, and now I must say good night.

TORVALD: Already? Is this knitting yours?

MRS. LINDE: *(picking it up)* Yes, thank you. I'd almost forgotten it.

TORVALD: So you knit?

MRS. LINDE: Of course.

TORVALD: You know, you ought to take up embroidery.

MRS. LINDE: Really? Why?

TORVALD: It's much more . . . becoming. Watch me. You hold the embroidery like this in your left hand, with the needle in your right—like this— making a long, graceful curve. Do you see?

MRS. LINDE: Yes. Perhaps—

TORVALD: Yes, but knitting! That will always be *un*becoming. Watch—your arms are close together, the needles go up and down—it looks sort of Chinese. They had really excellent champagne.

MRS. LINDE: Well, good night, Nora. Don't be stubborn anymore.

TORVALD: That's right, Mrs. Linde.

MRS. LINDE: Good night, Mr. Helmer.

TORVALD: *(walking her to the door)* Good night, good night. I hope you'll get home all right. I'd be very happy to—but you don't have far to go. Good night, good night. *(she goes out, he shuts the door after her, and comes back in)* Ah! At last! At last we've gotten rid of her. She's such an old bore, that woman.

NORA: Aren't you tired, Torvald?

TORVALD: Not in the least.

NORA: You're not sleepy?

TORVALD: Not at all. On the contrary, I feel full of life. And you? You look tired and quite sleepy.

NORA: Yes, I am very tired. I want to go to sleep right away.

TORVALD: There! I was right not to let you stay any longer.

NORA: Everything you do is right, Torvald.

TORVALD: *(kissing her on the forehead)* Finally my little lark is speaking the truth. Did you notice that Dr. Rank was in really good spirits tonight?

NORA: Really? Was he? I didn't talk to him at all.

TORVALD: I didn't say much to him. But I haven't seen him having such a good time for ages. *(look-*

ing at her for a while and then going nearer to her) It's delicious to be home again, all by ourselves, to be alone with you—you fascinating, lovely little creature.

NORA: Don't look at me like that, Torvald.

TORVALD: Why shouldn't I look at the thing I love most? All that beauty—and it's mine, all mine.

NORA: *(going to the other side of the table)* No, Torvald, you mustn't say things like that to me tonight.

TORVALD: *(following her)* I can see you've still got the tarantella in your blood. It makes you more captivating than ever. Listen, the guests are beginning to leave. *(in a lower voice)* Nora, soon the whole house will be quiet.

NORA: Yes. I hope so.

TORVALD: Yes, my own darling Nora. Do you know, when I'm out at a party with you, like tonight, do you know why I don't talk to you very much, stay away from you, and only occasionally cast a furtive glance in your direction? Do you know why? It's because I pretend to myself that we are secretly in love and you are my secret fiancée. And that no one knows there is anything at all between us.

NORA: Yes, yes. I know that you're thinking about me all the time.

TORVALD: And then, when we're leaving and I'm putting the shawl over your lovely young shoulders, on your beautiful neck, then I pretend to myself that you are my young bride. And that we've just come from our wedding, and that I'm bringing you home for the first time—and that I'm going to be alone with you for the first time—all alone with my shy little darling. This whole evening I've been longing only for you. When I watched the sensual movements of the tarantella, my blood was on fire. I couldn't stand it any longer, and that's why I brought you down so early.

NORA: Go now, Torvald. You must let me go. I don't want—

TORVALD: What? You must be joking! My little Nora, you don't want? I'm your husband, aren't I?

(a knock at the outer door)

NORA: *(with a start)* Did you hear that?

TORVALD: *(going into the hall)* Who is it?

DR. RANK: *(outside)* It's me. May I come in for a moment?

TORVALD: *(in an annoyed whisper)* Oh, what does he want now? *(aloud)* Can you wait a moment? *(unlocking the door)* Come in! It's kind of you not to just pass by.

DR. RANK: I thought I heard your voice. I felt that I'd like to drop in. *(quickly looking around the room)* Ah yes—these dear rooms that I know so well. You're very happy and cozy in here, you two.

TORVALD: I think you made yourself quite happy upstairs too.

DR. RANK: Very much so. And why shouldn't I? Why shouldn't I enjoy all the world has to offer—at least as much as I can for as long as I can. The wine was superb.

TORVALD: Especially the champagne.

DR. RANK: You noticed that too? I can hardly believe how much I managed to put away.

NORA: Torvald drank a large amount of champagne tonight too.

DR. RANK: Did he?

NORA: Yes. And he's always in such good spirits afterward.

DR. RANK: Well, why shouldn't you enjoy a happy evening after a hard day's work?

TORVALD: Hard day's work? I'm afraid I can't lay claim to that.

DR. RANK: *(clapping him on the back)* But *I* can.

NORA: Dr. Rank, have you been working on some scientific experiments?

DR. RANK: Exactly.

TORVALD: Listen to that. Little Nora talking about scientific experiments.

NORA: May I congratulate you on the result?

DR. RANK: Indeed you may.

NORA: It was favorable, then?

DR. RANK: Best possible result for both doctor and patient. Certainty.

NORA: *(quickly and inquiringly)* Certainty?

DR. RANK: Absolute certainty. So didn't I have the right to enjoy myself tonight?

NORA: Yes, you certainly did, Dr. Rank.

TORVALD: I agree. As long as you don't have to pay for it in the morning.

DR. RANK: Ah well, in this life nothing comes without a price.

NORA: Dr. Rank, do you enjoy these fancy dress balls?

DR. RANK: Yes, if there are lots of pretty costumes.

NORA: Tell me, what shall we two wear next year?

TORVALD: You little featherbrain! You're thinking about next year already?

DR. RANK: We two? Well, I can tell you. You will go as a guardian angel.

TORVALD: What do you think would be an appropriate costume for that?

DR. RANK: Your wife should go dressed as she is in everyday life.

TORVALD: That was a nice turn of phrase. But tell us what you would go as?

DR. RANK: Well, my dear friend, I've already made up my mind about that.

TORVALD: Well?

DR. RANK: At the next fancy dress ball I will be invisible.

TORVALD: That's very funny!

DR. RANK: I'll have a big black hat—did you ever hear of hats that make you invisible? If you put one on, nobody can see you.

TORVALD: *(suppressing a smile)* Yes, yes, quite right.

DR. RANK: But I'm totally forgetting what I came for. Torvald, give me a cigar. One of the black Havanas.

TORVALD: With the greatest of pleasure. *(offering him his case)*

DR. RANK: *(taking a cigar and cutting off the end)* Thank you.

NORA: *(striking a match)* Let me give you a light.

DR. RANK: Thank you. *(she holds the match for him to light the cigar)* And now, goodbye.

TORVALD: Goodbye, goodbye, you dear old man.

NORA: Sleep well, Dr. Rank.

DR. RANK: Thank you for the wish.

NORA: Wish me the same.

DR. RANK: You? Well, if that's what you want—sleep well. And thank you for the light. *(he nods to both of them and goes out)*

TORVALD: *(in a quiet voice)* He's drunk more than he should.

NORA: *(absently)* Perhaps. *(Torvald takes a bunch of keys out of his pocket and goes into the hall)* Torvald, what are you doing out there?

TORVALD: Emptying the letterbox. It's full. There'll be no room for the newspaper in the morning.

NORA: Are you going to work tonight?

TORVALD: You know very well that I'm not. What's this? Someone's been picking at the lock!

NORA: The lock?

TORVALD: Yes, someone's been . . . what's . . . ? I'm sure the maid wouldn't— Here's a broken hair-pin. Nora, it's one of yours.

NORA: *(quickly)* It must have been the children, then.

TORVALD: You must teach them not to do things like that. There, I've got it open. *(taking out the letters and calling out to the kitchen)* Helene! Helene! Put the front door light out. *(Comes back in the room, shuts the hall door. His hands are full of letters.)* Look at this. Look at this pile of letters. *(sorting through them)* What on earth is this?

NORA: *(at the window)* The letter. No, Torvald, no!

TORVALD: Two of Dr. Rank's cards.

NORA: Dr. Rank's?

TORVALD: *(looking at them)* Yes, they were on top. He must have put them in on his way out.

NORA: Did he write anything on them?

TORVALD: There's a black cross over his name. Look at that. That's so disturbing. It looks as if he were announcing his own death.

NORA: That's exactly what he's doing.

TORVALD: What? Do you know anything about this? Has he spoken to you?

NORA: Yes. He told me that when the cards arrived it would be his way of saying goodbye. He's going to lock himself away and die.

TORVALD: My poor old friend! Of course I knew we wouldn't have him with us for very long. But so soon! And he's hiding himself away like a wounded animal.

NORA: If it has to happen, it's best that it should be done without a word. Don't you think so, Torvald?

TORVALD: *(walking up and down)* He'd become part of our lives. I can't think of him as having left us.

He suffered and he was lonely. He was like a cloud, a dark background to our sunlit happiness. Well, perhaps it's for the best. For him anyway. *(standing still)* And perhaps it is for us too, Nora. We have only ourselves now. *(putting his arms around her)* My wife, my darling, I don't feel I can hold you tight enough. You know, Nora, I've often wished that you might be in some great danger, so that I could risk my life, everything, just for you.

NORA: *(disengaging herself and speaking in a firm, clear voice)* You must read your letters now, Torvald.

TORVALD: No, not tonight. I want to be with you. I want to be with my darling wife.

NORA: When your best friend is dying?

TORVALD: Yes, you're right. It's touched us both. Something ugly has come between us. The thought of mortality in all its horror. We must try to empty our minds of that. Until we do—we'll each go to our own room.

NORA: *(hanging on to his neck)* Good night, Torvald, good night.

TORVALD: *(kissing her on the forehead)* Good night, my little songbird. Sleep well, Nora. I'm going to read my letters. *(he takes the mail and goes into his study, shutting the door)*

NORA: *(groping around the room, picks up Torvald's cloak, throws it around her, speaking in quick, broken whispers)* Never to see him again. Never, never. *(putting her shawl over her head)* Never to see my children again—never again. Never, never—the black icy water—deep, deep down. If only it were all over. He's got it now and he's reading it.

Goodbye, Torvald. Goodbye, my children. *(she's about to rush out through the hall when Torvald opens his door quickly and stands with the letter in his hand)*

TORVALD: Nora!

NORA: Ah.

TORVALD: What's this? Do you know what's in this letter?

NORA: Yes, I know. Let me go. Let me get out of here.

TORVALD: *(holding her back)* Where are you going?

NORA: *(trying to get free)* You can't save me, Torvald.

TORVALD: *(staggering)* Is this true? Is this true? It's . . . horrible. No, no! It *can't* be true.

NORA: It is true. I have loved you more than anything else in the world.

TORVALD: Oh, don't give me any silly excuses.

NORA: *(stepping toward him)* Torvald.

TORVALD: You . . . miserable thing. What have you done?

NORA: Let me go. You're not going to suffer for my sake. You're not going to take this upon yourself.

TORVALD: Let's have no melodrama here. *(locking the hall door)* You're going to stay here and give me an explanation. Do you understand what you've done? Answer me! Do you understand what you've done?

NORA: *(looking steadily at him, with her face hardening)* Yes. I'm beginning to understand everything.

TORVALD: *(pacing around the room)* What a rude awakening. These eight years, she who was my pride

and joy was a hypocrite. A liar. No, worse, worse—
a criminal. It's so unspeakably awful. For shame,
for shame! *(Nora is silent and looks steadily at him.*
He stands in front of her.) I should have suspected
that something like this would happen. I
should've known. Your father's total lack of principle—don't interrupt—his total lack of principle
has finally come out in you. No religion, no
ethics, no sense of duty. I'm being punished now
for turning a blind eye to all that he did. And I
did that just for you. And this is how you repay
me.

NORA: Yes. This is how.

TORVALD: You've destroyed all my happiness. You've
ruined my future. I can't bear to think of it. I'm
in the hands of a man with no scruples. He can
do what he likes with me. He can ask anything he
wants, order me to do anything—and I dare not
say no. And I have to sink to such depths of
agony, all because of a thoughtless woman.

NORA: When I am gone, you will be free.

TORVALD: Don't play with words, please. Your father
was always very good at that. What good would it
do me if you were "gone," as you say? None at all.
He can tell the world about all this, and if he
does, I may be suspected, falsely, of having been a
partner in your crime. In fact, most people would
probably think that I was behind it—that it was I
who suggested it. And I have you to thank for all
of this. You, the one I have loved throughout our
married life. Do you understand what it is you
have done to me?

NORA: *(coldly and quietly)* Yes.

TORVALD: It's so hard to believe—I can't take it all in! But—you and I must come to some understanding. Take off that shawl. Take it off, I tell you! I must find a way of appeasing him. We've got to make sure that this business is hushed up, no matter the cost. As for you and me, we've got to make it look like everything between us is just as it was before. Naturally, that's only for the eyes of the world. You will still remain here in my house. That is taken for granted. But you will not be allowed to raise the children. I could not trust you with them. To think that I have to say that to someone I have loved so deeply—someone I still—no, that is all over. From this moment on, it's not a question of happiness. All there is now is saving what's left of our shattered lives, keeping up appearances. *(front doorbell rings, Torvald jumps)* What's that? At this time? It can't get any worse, he can't . . . Keep out of sight, Nora. Say you're ill. *(Nora does not move. Torvald goes and unlocks the hall door. The Maid, half dressed, comes to the door.)*

MAID: A letter for the mistress.

TORVALD: Give it to me. *(he takes the letter and shuts the door)* It's from him. You can't have it—I'll read it myself.

NORA: Yes, read it.

TORVALD: *(standing by the lamp)* I can hardly bring myself to do it. This could be the ruin of us both. No, I have to know. *(he tears open the letter, reads a few lines, looks at a piece of paper enclosed, and gives a shout)* Nora! *(she looks at him with questions in her eyes)* Nora! No, I've got to read it again. It's true! Yes, I'm saved. Nora, I'm saved!

NORA: And I?

TORVALD: You too, of course. We're both saved. The two of us. Look! He's sent you the contract back. He says that he's sorry. He apologizes . . . there's a happy change of events in his life. Oh, never mind what he says . . . we're saved, Nora! No one can do anything to you. Oh, Nora, Nora—no, first I must destroy these terrible things. Let me see . . . *(looking at the contract)* No, no, I don't want to look at it. The whole thing will be nothing but a bad dream. *(tears up the contract and the letters, throws them into the stove, and watches them burn)* There. Now they're gone forever. He said that since Christmas Eve . . . you . . . these past three days must have been agonizing for you, Nora.

NORA: I've been fighting a hard battle.

TORVALD: And you must have suffered. There was no way out except—but no, we mustn't think about all the horror you went through. All we must do is shout with joy and keep telling each other it's over, it's over! Listen to me, Nora, you don't seem to understand that it's all over. What's the matter?—such a cold, hard face. Oh my poor Nora, I quite understand. You can hardly believe that I have forgiven you. But it's true, Nora, I swear to you. I've forgiven you. Totally. I know that what you did you did because you love me.

NORA: That is true.

TORVALD: You loved me as a wife should love her husband. You were just too naive to understand the implications of what you were doing. But do you think I love you the less because you didn't understand how to do things on your own? No, no. You must rely on me. I will advise you and give you directions. I wouldn't be a man if this fe-

107

male helplessness didn't make you twice as attractive to me. You must forget the harsh things I said when I was so upset at first. I thought my whole world was collapsing about me. I have forgiven you, Nora. I swear to you, I have forgiven you.

NORA: Thank you for forgiving me. *(she goes out through the door on the right)*

TORVALD: No, don't go— *(looking in)* What are you doing in there?

NORA: *(inside)* Taking off my costume.

TORVALD: *(standing by the open door)* Yes. Do that. Try to calm yourself down. Put your mind at ease, my frightened little songbird. You're safe now, and my big broad wings will protect you. *(walking to and fro by the door)* Nora, our home is so warm and cozy. Here you will always be safe. I will protect you—like a hunted dove that I've saved from the talons of a hawk. I will calm your poor beating heart. Little by little it will happen. Trust me, Nora. Tomorrow morning you'll think about it quite differently. Soon everything will be as it was before. In no time you won't need me to assure you that I have forgiven you. You will be absolutely sure that I have. Surely you can't imagine that I would reject you or even reproach you? You can't imagine what a real man's heart is like, Nora. It is so indescribably sweet and satisfying for a man to know that he has forgiven his wife— completely forgiven her and with all his heart. It's as if that simple act has made her doubly his own. It's as if he had given her a new life. And so, in a way she is now both wife and child to him. That is what you will be for me from now on, little frightened helpless darling. You mustn't worry about anything, Nora. All you have to do is be open, frank, and honest with me, and I will be the conscience and the will for you and . . . What's this? Not in bed? You've changed.

NORA: *(in her everyday clothes)* Yes, Torvald, I've changed.

TORVALD: But why?— It's so late.

NORA: I won't go to sleep tonight.

TORVALD: But my dear Nora—

NORA: *(looking at her watch)* It's not that late. Sit down, Torvald. You and I have a lot to say to each other. *(she sits down at one side of the table)*

TORVALD: Nora—what's this?—your eyes are so cold!

NORA: Sit down. This will take some time; we have a lot to talk about.

TORVALD: *(sits down at the opposite side of the table)* You're frightening me, Nora!—I don't understand you.

NORA: No, that's just it. You don't understand me, and I've never understood you either—until tonight. No, you mustn't interrupt me. I want you to just listen to what I have to say. Torvald, it's time we settled our accounts.

TORVALD: What do you mean by that?

NORA: *(after a short silence)* Doesn't anything strike you as strange in our sitting here like this?

TORVALD: What would that be?

NORA: We've been married now for eight years. Do you realize that this is the first time that we two, you and I, man and wife, have had a serious conversation?

TORVALD: What do you mean serious?

NORA: In all these eight years—no, longer than that—from the moment we first met, we have never exchanged a *word* on any serious subject.

TORVALD: Well, why would I keep on talking to you about my worries? There was nothing you could do to help.

NORA: I'm not talking about business. What I'm saying is that we have never really sat down together to try and get to the bottom of anything.

TORVALD: But, my dear Nora, what good would that have done you?

NORA: That's just it. You have never understood me. I have been greatly wronged, Torvald—first by Papa and then by you.

TORVALD: What! By your father and me? —the two men who loved you more than anyone else in the world?

NORA: *(shaking her head)* You have never loved me. You just thought it was pleasant to be *in* love with me.

TORVALD: Nora, what are you saying?

NORA: It's perfectly true, Torvald. When I was at home with Papa, he gave me his opinions on everything. So I had the same opinions as he did. If I disagreed with him I concealed the fact, because he wouldn't have liked it. He called me his doll-child, and he played with me just as I used to play with my dolls. And when I came to live in your house—

TORVALD: What a way to talk about our marriage!

NORA: *(undisturbed)* I mean that I was simply handed over from Papa to you. You arranged everything to suit your own tastes, and so I had the same tastes as you—or else I pretended to. I'm really not sure which—I think sometimes the one and sometimes the other. When I look back on it, it seems to me that I was living here like a pauper—from hand to mouth. The whole reason for my existence was to perform tricks for you, Torvald. But that's what you wanted. You and Papa have committed a great sin against me. It is your fault that I have made nothing of my life.

TORVALD: How unreasonable and how ungrateful, Nora! Haven't you been happy here?

NORA: No, I have never been happy. I thought I was, but I haven't been.

TORVALD: Not—happy!

NORA: No. Just cheerful. You have always been so kind to me. But our home has been nothing but a playroom. I have been your doll-wife, just as at home I was Papa's doll-child; and in this house the children have been my dolls. I thought it was great fun when you played with me, and they thought it was great fun when I played with them. That is what our marriage has been, Torvald.

TORVALD: There's some truth in what you say—though you've exaggerated and made too much of it. But in the future things will be different. Playtime is over, and it's time for lessons.

NORA: Whose lessons? Mine or the children's?

TORVALD: Yours *and* the children's, Nora, my darling.

NORA: I'm sorry, Torvald, but you are not the man to teach me how to be a proper wife to you.

TORVALD: How can you say that!

NORA: And how am I fit to bring up the children?

TORVALD: Nora!

NORA: Didn't you say yourself a little while ago—that you dare not trust me to bring them up?

TORVALD: That was in a moment of anger! Why do you pay any attention to that?

NORA: No, you were perfectly right. I am not fit to bring them up. There is something else I must do first. I must try to educate myself—and you are not the man to help me do that. I must do that by myself. That is why I am leaving you.

TORVALD: *(springing up)* What did you say?

NORA: I must be by myself if I'm going to understand myself and the world around me. That is why I can't stay with you any longer.

TORVALD: Nora, Nora!

NORA: I am leaving, right away. I'm sure Kristine will take me in for the night—

TORVALD: You're out of your mind! I won't allow it! I forbid you!

NORA: There's no point in forbidding me anything any longer. I'll take with me only what belongs to me. I'll take nothing from you—now or later.

TORVALD: What kind of mad behavior is this?

NORA: Tomorrow I will go home—to my old home, I mean. It will be easier for me to find something to do there.

TORVALD: You foolish woman! You can't see what you're doing!

NORA: I must try and make some sense of all this, Torvald.

TORVALD: You're deserting your home, your husband, and your children! Think what people will say!

NORA: I can't think about that at all. All I know is that I have no other option.

TORVALD: I am deeply shocked. Is this how you neglect your most sacred duties?

NORA: What do you think are my most sacred duties?

TORVALD: Do I need to tell you? Your duty to your husband and your children!

NORA: I have another duty just as sacred.

TORVALD: No, you don't. What duty could that be?

NORA: My duty to myself.

TORVALD: Before everything else, you are a wife and a mother.

NORA: I don't believe that any more. I believe that before everything I am a thinking human being, just as you are—or, at any rate, that I must try to become one. I know very well, Torvald, that most people would think you are right, and that your views would be supported in books. But I can no longer be satisfied with what most people say or what's written in books. I must think things over for myself and try to understand them.

TORVALD: Why not try to understand your place in your own home? Haven't you got a dependable guide in things like—your religion?

NORA: I'm afraid, Torvald, I don't really know what religion is.

TORVALD: What are you saying?

NORA: All I know is what my pastor told me when I was confirmed. He told us that religion was this, that, and the other. When I have left all this behind, when I am alone, I will look into that too. I will find out if what the pastor said is true, or at least if it is true for me.

TORVALD: This is unheard of in a girl like you! But if religion can't put you on the right path, then let me try to prick your conscience. You have *some* moral sense, don't you? Or—now answer me—am I supposed to think that you don't?

NORA: Well, Torvald, that is not an easy question to answer. I really don't know. I am totally perplexed. All I know is that you and I look at it very differently. And I am finding out too that the law is very different from what I thought. I find it impossible to convince myself that the law is right. According to the law, a woman has no right to protect her old and dying father, or to save her husband's life. I can't believe that.

TORVALD: You're talking like a child. You don't understand the world we live in.

NORA: No, I don't. But I intend to try. I'm going to find out which is right, the world or I.

TORVALD: You are not well, Nora, you must have a fever. I almost think you may be out of your mind.

NORA: My mind has never been so clear and determined as tonight.

TORVALD: And with this clear mind of yours you are determined to abandon your husband and your children?

114

NORA: Yes.

TORVALD: Then there is only one possible explanation.

NORA: What?

TORVALD: You do not love me anymore.

NORA: No, that is just it.

TORVALD: Nora!—how can you say that?

NORA: It's very painful, Torvald. You have always been so kind to me, but I can't help it. I don't love you anymore.

TORVALD: *(regaining his composure)* Are you clear and determined about that too?

NORA: Yes, absolutely clear and determined. That is why I won't stay here any longer.

TORVALD: And can you tell me what I have done to lose your love?

NORA: Yes, I can. It was tonight, when the miracle didn't happen. It was then that I saw you were not the man I thought you were.

TORVALD: Please explain yourself—I don't understand.

NORA: I had waited so patiently for eight years. Goodness knows, I didn't think that miracles happen every day. Then this . . . this . . . disaster fell upon me, and I felt quite sure that the miracle was finally going to happen. When Krogstad's letter was in the mailbox, never for a moment did I think you would accept his conditions. I was absolutely sure that you would say to him: Go ahead! Publish it. Let the whole world know! And after that—

TORVALD: Yes, what then?—after I had exposed my wife to shame and disgrace?

NORA: After that—I was absolutely sure that you would step forward and assume all the blame and say, "I am the guilty one."

TORVALD: Nora—!

NORA: What you are thinking is that I would never have accepted a sacrifice like that from you. No, of course I wouldn't. But what would my word have been against yours? That was the miracle I was hoping for. The miracle I was afraid of. It was to make sure that did not happen that I was ready to kill myself.

TORVALD: I would slave night and day for you, Nora—I would endure sorrow and poverty for your sake. But no man would sacrifice his honor even for the one he loves.

NORA: Thousands of women have done that.

TORVALD: You're thinking and talking like a stupid child.

NORA: Perhaps. But you don't think or talk like the man I could spend the rest of my life with. As soon as you stopped being frightened—and you weren't afraid of what was happening to me, you were afraid of what was happening to you—when it was over, as far as you were concerned it was just as if nothing had happened. Exactly as before, I was your little lark. I was your doll. Of course you would handle it twice as gently. It was so delicate and fragile. *(getting up)* Torvald—it was then it dawned on me that for eight years I've been living with a stranger and I had borne him three children—. Oh, I can't bear to think of it! I could tear myself to pieces!

116

TORVALD: *(sadly)* Yes. I see, I see. A gulf has opened up between us—I see that now. But Nora, couldn't we bridge that gulf?

NORA: The woman I am now is no wife for you.

TORVALD: I could change who I am—

NORA: Perhaps—if your doll is taken away from you.

TORVALD: But to lose you!—to lose you forever! No, no, Nora, I can't accept that.

NORA: *(going out to the right)* That is why it must happen. *(she comes back with her cloak and hat and a small bag which she puts on a chair by the table)*

TORVALD: Nora. Nora, not now! Wait until tomorrow.

NORA: *(putting on her cloak)* I can't spend the night in the house of a stranger.

TORVALD: But we could live here like brother and sister—?

NORA: *(putting on her hat)* You know that that wouldn't last. *(puts the cloak round her)* Goodbye, Torvald. I won't see my children. I know they're in better hands than mine. The woman I am now would be no use to them.

TORVALD: But someday, Nora—someday?

NORA: How can I answer that? I've no idea of what's going to become of me.

TORVALD: But you are my wife, whatever happens to you.

NORA: Listen, Torvald. I have heard that when a wife leaves her husband's house, as I am doing now, he is legally freed from all obligations toward her. In any case, *I* am setting you free. You're not to

117

feel like a prisoner in any way. I will not feel that way at all. There must be perfect freedom on both sides. Here is your ring back. Give me mine.

TORVALD: That too?

NORA: That too.

TORVALD: Here it is.

NORA: There. Now it's all over. I've put the keys here. The maids know all about running the house—much better than I do. Tomorrow, after I've left, Kristine will come and pack the things I brought with me from home. I'll have them sent on to me.

TORVALD: It's all over! All over!—Nora, will you never think of me again?

NORA: I know that I will often think of you . . . and the children . . . and this house.

TORVALD: May I write to you, Nora?

NORA: No—never. You must never do that.

TORVALD: But at least let me send you—

NORA: Nothing—nothing—

TORVALD: Just let me help you if you ever need it.

NORA: No. I can never accept anything from a stranger.

TORVALD: Nora—can I never be anything more than a stranger to you?

NORA: *(taking her bag)* Oh, Torvald, the greatest miracle of all would have to happen.

TORVALD: What would that be?

NORA: You and I would have to change so much that—. Oh, Torvald, I don't believe in miracles anymore.

TORVALD: But I will. Tell me!—changed so much that—?

NORA: That our life together would be a real marriage. Goodbye. *(she goes out through the hall)*

TORVALD: *(sinks down on a chair at the door and buries his face in his hands)* Nora! Nora! *(looks round and rises)* Empty. She's gone. *(a glimmer of hope flashes across his face)* The greatest miracle of all—?

(the sound of a door shutting is heard from below)